GOING TOO FAR

Essays About America's Nervous Breakdown

Also by Ishmael Reed

Ishmael Reed

GOING TOO FAR

Essays About America's Nervous Breakdown

Baraka
Books
Montreal

Library and Archives Canada Cataloguing in Publication

Reed, Ishmael, 1938-

   Going too far: essays about America's nervous breakdown / Ishmael Reed.
   Also issued in electronic format.

   ISBN 978-1-926824-56-7

   1. African Americans–Social conditions–21st century. 2. African Americans in popular
   culture. 3. United States–Race relations. 4. Racism–United States. I. Title.

E185.86.R43 2012   305.896'073   C2012-905245-0

Cover cartoon by Ishmael Reed
Back cover photo: Tennessee Reed
Cover and book design by Folio Infographie

Legal Deposit, 3rd quarter, 2012
Bibliothèque et Archives nationales du Québec
Library and Archives Canada

Published by Baraka Books of Montreal.
6977, rue Lacroix
Montréal, Québec H4E 2V4
Telephone: 514 858-6333, extension 226
info@barakabooks.com
www.barakabooks.com

Printed and bound in Quebec
Trade Distribution & Returns
United States
Independent Publishers Group
1-800-888-4741 (IPG1);

orders@ipgbook.com
Canada
LitDistCo
1-800-591-6250; ordering@litdistco.ca

Dedicated to Thelma V. Reed
June 2, 1917 to March 6, 2012

Author of *Black Girl From Tannery Flats*

"For unless you do your own acting and write your own plays,
your theatre will be of no use; it will in fact vulgarize and degrade you".

George Bernard SHAW

Contents

Going There

When they tell me "don't go there" that's my signal to navigate the forbidden topics of American life. Just as the ex-slaves were able to challenge the prevailing attitudes about race in the United States after arriving in Canada, I am able to argue from Quebec against ordained opinion that paints the United States as a place where the old sins of racism have been vanquished and that those who insist that much work remains to be done are involved in "Old Fights," as one of my young critics, John McWhorter, claims in articles in *Commentary* and *The New Republic*, where I am dismissed as an out of touch "fading anachronism." Benjamin Drew recorded the testimony of fugitive slaves, who, from Canada, challenged the prevailing opinion in the United States that slaves were content under the management of merciful slave masters. In *The Refugee: Narratives of the Fugitive Slaves in Canada*, he wrote: "Their enemies, the supporters of slavery, have represented them as 'indolent, vicious, and debased; suffering and starving,' because they have no kind masters to do the thinking for them, and to urge them to the necessary labor, which their own laziness and want of forecast, lead them to avoid."

I was struck by the fact that some of the same issues confronting Drew's 1851 generation are contemporary. Since the ushering in of right-wing administrations, beginning with Ronald Reagan, the wealthy have been financing foundations staffed with intellectuals

and academics who have issued a number of books and papers proposing that whichever problems faced by what they refer to as "the
underclass," are caused by their "laziness," and "idleness." Rick
Santelli, who refers to himself as the Tea Party's "lightning rod," and
the former presidential candidate Rick Santorum have used the
argument of black dependency as career moves, the kind of stereotype that is still aimed at Italian Americans.

Santelli says that Tea Partiers are angry because minorities are
receiving all of the entitlements, when a recent study showed that
the entitlements are being hogged up by the Red States, where most
Tea Party members reside.

For his part, Santorum accused blacks of ripping off money from
white people, when it would take a few hundred years for blacks and
Hispanics to catch up with the kind of government and private sec-
tor favoritism that whites have received. The line that the problems
of blacks are self-inflicted is subscribed to by some media, academic
and artistic blacks, whose opinions and roles are managed by their
sponsors whether it be Lionsgate, a studio that produced *Precious,*
or MSNBC, which actually has an ex-Santorum black speechwriter
as a regular. Though the support for Republican presidential candidates runs at about two percent among blacks, Michael Steele, a
former black chair of the Republican National Committee wanders
from studio to studio all day on MSNBC to offer commentary
against the president.

A younger generation of black commentators and writers propose
that black nationalists have hampered their ability to express themselves. I made the same argument in the 1960s and 70s until I realized that black nationalists didn't have the power to impede my
expressions as a writer. Black nationalists don't have the power to
prevent Touré from enjoying Beethoven or John McWhorter from
enjoying Verdi.

It was with the advent of the white middle class feminist movement, a powerful ally of corporate patriarchy, that my problems with
censorship began. Some members of the younger generation also
accuse me of being a curmudgeon and a crank and that my prob-

lems with the police for example have been exaggerated or made up all together, yet there are members of their generation who see it differently. Alex Maynard, an actor, and son of the late Robert Maynard, the first black publisher of a major newspaper, was beaten by members of the notorious New York Police Department, whose fascist measures against blacks led to the exodus of blacks from the city. Adam Kennedy, the son of the great playwright Adrienne Kennedy, was beaten by police in his front yard.

These young post-black and post-race writers, whose leader is "intellectual entrepreneur" Henry Louis Gates, Jr., have even convinced economist Paul Krugman that Jim Crow is dead. Apparently Paul Krugman hasn't read his newspaper, which has printed accounts of the Bank of America and other banks settling lawsuits whose plaintiffs accuse them of discriminating against black and Hispanic borrowers. A post-black proponent, Touré, who told an audience at a Washington D.C. club called Busboys and Poets, that racism is no longer "overt," doesn't read the newspaper for which he is a contributor, *The New York Times*, which publishes studies and reports frequently showing that blatant racism is still a problem against which blacks must struggle, daily, whether they are a black youth murdered because he was found walking in a gated community, or the black superintendent of New York schools, who got harassed by two New York policemen. Here are some examples of blatant Nazi-like experiments that are only covert because a media that criticizes China for its alleged human rights abuses ignores them and media commentators like Touré are restricted from talking about them. Here is one of the "old fights" that I consider important: the continued use of blacks and poor people as guinea pigs, which has been reported on regularly. * (See note at the end of the Introduction.)

Not only does blatant racism like these Mengele-like experiments still exist, reminding us that the Nazis learned from the U.S. eugenics movement, which succeeded in getting poor people sterilized, but black access to the ballot box, the issue over which hundreds of blacks lost their lives, is being challenged in a number of states. This is part of a plan promoted by the American Legislative Exchange

Council (ALEC), a foundation supported by corporate sponsors, whose aim is to diminish the black vote in order to defeat a black president. These discussions are deemed off limits by the media from which most Americans receive information. I've watched dozens of panels in which every motive is ascribed to the president's opponents except racism. The producers believe that such a topic would alienate their target audience, which Rick Sanchez, former CNN anchor, described as "angry white males." Because he was fired, he had nothing to lose by being candid.

Just as there was a consensus between Northern and Southern whites, a consensus criticized by Frederick Douglass, who saw the rise of a pro Southern literature as an unsettling trend, an alliance between progressives and the far right is beginning to form.

I predicted that such an alliance would begin in my book, *Barack Obama and the Jim Crow Media, The Return of the Nigger Breakers.* The title of that book is still apt. A recent PEW study reports that of all of the presidential candidates the president has received the most unfavorable treatment by the media. Both CNN and MSNBC have formed an alliance with the Tea Party, which includes leaders who've called for the president's assassination. Even Melissa Harris-Perry, a black woman, described by MSNBC as a progressive, said that "There are a lot of things I like about the Tea Party." What lot of things? A prominent Tea Party member referred to the president as "a skunk," a reference to the president's bi-racial heritage. Does she like the Tea Partiers showing up at rallies with guns, or signs showing the president in a coffin? Calling for his assassination? Jules Manson, a darling of the Tea Party, made a Facebook post that said the following: "Assassinate the fucken nigger and his monkey children."

And so while the media, both electronic and print, might peddle the mass delusion that racism is no longer a factor in American life, I can offer a different witness because, unlike many black men who might entertain the same idea, I have many outlets, both here and abroad, both from mainstream, alternative media and my own, and so while the average American reviewer didn't have a clue about what to make of my novel *Japanese By Spring,* Chinese universities selected it as a national project. In order to survive, I had to become a world-class writer.

Some of the essays in this book have drawn sharp, testy responses from those who have greater access to the mainstream media than I. But as in the case of my being quoted in *The New Yorker*, where my letter contextualizing the quote wasn't published, Joan Walsh's reply to my *Times* Op-Ed caused a furor by critics who said that she misinterpreted my Op-Ed that was critical of progressives and that she refused to provide a link to my essay, but the controversy led to her being given gentle treatment by *The AtlanticWire* and the nationally televised show *Reliable Sources*. At no time during the show or at *The AtlanticWire* site was there any mention of the fact that my Op-Ed was the origin of the controversy.

Some progressives are upset with me because I disagree with them that the Tea Party, which arose from the seedy imagination of Roger Ailes, president of Fox News, and creator of the Willie Horton ad, and the billionaire Koch brothers, is a populist uprising against Wall Street. Another Willie Horton alumnae, Larry McCarthy, has been signed up for one of the Super PACs supporting Mitt Romney. Jane Mayer did a profile of this character in *The New Yorker* (13 February 2012): "McCarthy's detailed résumé, posted on the Web site of his advertising company, omits his most notorious creation—the Willie Horton ad. Paid for by a political group officially acting separately from the campaign of George H. W. Bush, it was the political equivalent of an improvised explosive device, demolishing the electoral hopes of Dukakis, then the governor of Massachusetts. Its key image was a mug shot of Horton—a scowling black man with a disheveled Afro. Horton, a convicted murderer, had escaped while on a weekend pass issued by a Massachusetts furlough program. A decade earlier, Dukakis had vetoed a bill that would have forbidden furloughs for murderers. After escaping, Horton raped a white woman and stabbed her fiancé. McCarthy knew that showing Horton's menacing face would make voters feel viscerally that Dukakis was soft on crime. Critics said that the ad stoked racial fears, presenting a little-known black man as an icon of American violence."

Progressives believe that class trumps race in determining the status of a person in American society, which doesn't explain why whites, regardless of their credit ratings, have easier access to loans than middle class blacks with a credit rating at 800. One of my brothers whom most would consider wealthy had problems obtaining a mortgage, and I've written about my ordeal with the banks in *The New York Times*. Though progressives still cling to a fantasy to which they've been attached since at least the 1920s, that class determines one's status in American society, to millions of whites, we are all underclass. Notice how images hostile to the president show him as an underclass hoodlum, or associate him with food stamps, or fast foods like KFC, or on an email circulated by a candidate for governor of New York, a pimp and his wife a whore. The president and his wife are graduates of one of their top elite schools.

Both black and white progressives have criticized my defense of the president. The black ones seem to want President Obama to be Malcolm X, the white ones, Castro. In comparison to the president's support among Democrats, blacks and Hispanics, these progressives constitute a fringe movement, but because they have access to print and electronic media, whose aim is to defeat the president, this fringe movement poses as the president's "base," when the momentum for the president's winning the election began in Iowa, voters whom the progressive elite would consider hayseeds.

In the first essay in this book, "President Obama and the New Secession," I am able to present a different view of why the opposition to a black president is so tenacious between both elements of the white right and the left. In my first book published by Baraka Books, I predicted that the progressives and the right would form an alliance. This alliance has occurred as some progressives call for a unification of Tea Party forces and the Occupy Movement, a white led movement, which has been criticized by minority groups for ignoring their causes. (This of course isn't the first time that someone deemed a neo-liberal has entertained a right wing idea. Newt Gingrich's idea of putting black kids to work as janitors in schools was first proposed by Joe Klein, a man who believes his moral values to be superior to those of black inner city residents, yet lied about his authorship of *Primary Colors*). I addressed the Occupy's alienation from the black movement in my "Trouble By The Bay," in which I argued that the Oakland occupation had overshadowed local issues important to blacks. This comment has since then been echoed by other black commentators including one of the more brilliant of the younger generation of writers, Ta-Nehisi Coates, senior editor at *The Atlantic*.

Other progressives warmed to the candidacy of Ron Paul, who once edited a racist and anti-Semitic newsletter. Appearing on KPFA radio, one said that the white led Occupy Movement should join the white led Tea Party on the basis of "shared premises." And get this: Arianna Huffington, who shifts from left to right so frequently that watching her is like watching a tennis match, praised Andrew Breitbart, the late frothing-at-the-mouth right-winger who lied about Sherry Sherrod and might end up destroying the legacy of the late Derrick Bell of Harvard. She's frustrated with Barack Obama and called his taking credit for capturing Osama bin Laden "despicable." I see the Tea Party differently from those who embrace it on TV including Melissa Harris-Perry. I see the Tea Party's take over of Congress as being as scary as the Nazi Party's take over of the German parliament in the 1930s, and for those who might protest that such an analogy is off limits, I would remind progressives that prominent neo-Nazis and Holocaust deniers play an important role in the Tea Party.

One prominent Tea Party member called for the president's assassination. I express my dismay about the rise of the Tea Party in the essays "Brown Shirts, Black Shirts, T-Shirts," "Ethnic Studies in the Age of the Tea Party," and "A Fly on the Wall."

The title of the first Baraka Books publication, *Barack Obama and the Jim Crow Media, The Return of the Nigger Breakers*, addressed the depletion of minority representation and points of view, a depletion which, according to Richard Prince, a media watcher, has accelerated. CNN has actually joined forces with the Tea Party by co-sponsoring a debate with the Tea Party Express, which is led by

a man who has made crazy statements about the president. Further
proof that the country is suffering a nervous breakdown is the sight
of a bishop—who when presiding over the Catholic Church in
Milwaukee was considered unsympathetic to victims of abuse—
being able to intimidate the president over the issue of contraception
without the media mentioning his scandalous behavior in
Milwaukee. In the first book, I mentioned the difference between
the coverage of Rev. Jeremiah Wright and that of Pope Benedict,
whose arrival in New York was celebrated by the media with much
affection. Since the publication of *Barack Obama and the Jim Crow
Media* there has been an effort to try the Pope in the courts for
human rights abuses. This charge arises from his covering up the
pedophilia scandal when cardinal.

The media is still hammering Rev. Wright. If a country believes
that making a strong sermon is a more serious violation than Bishop
Timothy Dolan, now a cardinal, harboring pedophiles, what does
that say about the country? If a gun lobby is a special interest group
that has more power than the church, what does that say about the
country? If over fifty percent of the South believe that the president
is a Muslim and was born in Kenya, a case of mass hysteria, what
does that say about the state of mind of millions of the country's
inhabitants? If big pharma is still carrying out sinister experiments
on unsuspecting orphans, the poor, blacks and prisoners, doesn't
this reflect the country's state of mind? Millions of Tea Party voters
elected Tea Party representatives who then threatened the portfolios
and pensions of these same voters by indulging in a wild stunt that
resulted in the country's credit rating being lowered by Standard
and Poor's. Isn't it crazy that these voters would risk their retirement
savings because a black president was elected, a president toward
whom they hold great enmity?

And so for me, the president is not a Muslim. He is more like the
Catholic priest, Father Merrin, played by Max von Sydow in the
movie *The Exorcist,* who tends to the possessed girl, Regan MacNeil,
played by Linda Blair, because his being president has gushed up all
of the racist bile like that green stuff flowing from Linda Blair's

mouth. Ugly, vicious and shocking cartoons have appeared of a racist nature about the president and his family, not just from the typical yahoos, but from a candidate for Governor in the state of New York. It was a federal judge who thought it was funny to show the president's mother as someone who had sexual intercourse with a dog. At a party. But instead of producing projects that heal, Hollywood and the corporate media play to stereotypes about blacks, a big money maker since the beginning of the film and newspaper industry.

The film *Precious,* which was produced by a studio, Lionsgate, which, like the Oscar's Board of Governors, has no blacks among its executive leadership, could be used as campaign material for a Tea Party candidate with its portrait of conniving lay-abouts, welfare cheats, a black male as a sexual beast, and even an image that invokes the stock minstrel gag of blacks as chicken thieves. I received some of the most vitriolic criticism of my career for challenging the white producers' motives in my essays "The Selling of *Precious,*" "Fade to White" and "The NAACP's House of Shame," which refers to the NAACP rewarding this film which advocates the sterilization of poor black women. Walter White, a former NAACP executive who in the 1940s sought to encourage the studios to produce films that would depict blacks as more than buffoons and maids, would turn over in his grave at the sight of the NAACP handing out awards to black boogeyman films in exchange for donations.

Among the white population what has been called pathology porn about blacks is in such demand that one of the more odious products about black life, *The Wire,* is being taught in American universities with droves of white students competing for space in the classrooms where *The Wire,* produced by David Simon, is listed on the syllabus. Maybe these are the same white students, who, inspired by David Simon's warped view of black life, amuse themselves with "ghetto" and "barrio" parties, or heckle black students with taunts invoking the name of Trayvon Martin. This incident occurred on the campus of Cornell University. So instead of reading works by Wright, Troupe, Marshall, Nunez, and Brooks, they get *The Wire,* which presents a distorted view of drug distribution and consumption. My essay, "The

Wire Goes to College" drew letters from two of the professors who were using *The Wire* in the classroom. Since the publication of that article, one of the show's writers, Richard Price, on the suggestion of CBS's Jane Rosenthal, has turned a novel-in-progress about Harlem into a new series called *NYC-22*. This comes at an appropriate time for the NYPD, now involved in scandals around its policy of "Stop and Frisk," which has singled out blacks and Hispanics for searches without cause, a Gestapo-like policy, which has been endorsed by New York Mayor Bloomberg, and managed by Police Commissioner Kelley. *The Village Voice* has exposed a scandal in a Brooklyn precinct in which the police engaged in capricious arrests of blacks as a way of filling quotas. The whistleblower, Adil Polanco, said, "They teach us to lie about stopping people. They teach us to lie about tickets, and ruin lives." The police harassed the whistleblower who revealed this scandal. In the 1990s, thirty police were charged with corruption in one Harlem precinct alone. Will any of this appear in the television series based upon the novel written by Richard Price, who has made so much money marketing what his supporters at *The New York Times* refer to as "urban disintegration" that he's moved to Harlem, where he's now leading tours of black landmarks?

For this tour, the *Times* has passed over black intellectuals and artists who've lived in Harlem for decades, including Quincy Troupe, former Poet Laureate of California, and publisher of *Black Renaissance Noire*, who has lived in Harlem for decades. When I criticized *The Wire*, David Simon, a "lord" behind the "urban disintegration" racket, said I was against him because he was a white man, ignoring the fact that I have published scores of white men and women over the years and some of whom, who are now famous, I was the first to publish. I said I was opposed to *The Wire*, because it was a cliché. Now that Neil Genzlinger has said the same thing about *The Wire*'s look-alike, or should it be called side effect, *NYC-22*, which received the blessings of Price's *Wire* colleague David Simon, are they going to say that Genzlinger is against Richard Price peddling this junk because he's white? Genzlinger calls the "urban disintegration" number an "exhausted genre." (Similarly, Sapphire, whose book *Push* was produced by Hollywood under the title *Precious,* said that I was "mentally ill" and jealous of black women who were receiving prizes, for criticizing the movie made from her book, yet a black reviewer, Danielle Evans, accused her of trafficking in "tragedy porn." Is she jealous of black women who've received prizes? Is she "mentally ill?")

Genzlinger adds, "The show may not help Harlem's efforts to improve its image. Gangs, drugs, robberies and arsons abound." I also criticized *The Wire* because it locates drug activities almost exclusively among the black population, which makes it propaganda, because, as writer Michelle Alexander told Sasha Lilley on the program *Against the Grain,* broadcast on KPFA radio, most drug users and sellers are white.

She said that a drug user in the rural mid-West isn't going to a Detroit ghetto to buy drugs. She blames media "saturation" which identifies blacks as typical drug users and salespersons for 95 *percent* of respondents to a survey identifying blacks as typical drug users and sellers. David Simon, Richard Price and George Pelecanos contribute to these perceptions, which promote stereotypes and influence public policy.

On April 17, 2012, a *Times* editorial mentioned that, "the majority of crack users are white and Hispanic, but as the sentencing commission reported, in 2010, blacks made up more than three-fourths of those sentenced under federal crack cocaine laws. Most were low-level offenders. The high number of black defendants and the disparity in treatment of crack versus powdered cocaine led federal sentences for blacks to jump to almost 50 percent higher than for whites in 1990." I've been writing about social pathology among the white population for years, but you won't see a CBS series about white meth or crack use, or a white version of *The Wire,* the kind of propaganda statement that the Nazis used to peddle about blacks. Director Debra Granik is one of the few white film directors who covers the use of meth in white rural communities, yet no courses exist that are devoted to the study of her film, *Winter's Bone.*

Those who have been annoyed by my criticism of Steven Spielberg's *The Color Purple* and other Hollywood films which market black degeneracy, claim that at least these films provide black actors with jobs. So did *Birth of a Nation*! Using a cynical marketing strategy, the producers of pathology porn movies like *The Help* offer an account of the civil rights struggle that departs from the one experienced by blacks and absolve from blame the group to which the producers, the director and the script writer belong, namely white men, many of whom terrorized blacks from the time they were sold as slaves until now. These white producers profit from the black boogeyman stereotype, a cash cow for television, the movies and chic lit, which critic C. Leigh McInnis claims "sells better than sex." This entertainment has black men carrying the burden for the male species as cruel to women. You even have Caitlin Flanagan, protégé of *Atlantic* editor, Benjamin Schwarz, who said that black men who were lynched in the South probably deserved it, commenting about black men being cruel to their wives. Maybe we can get some Irish American men to write an instruction manual about how to treat women.

Just as some white entrepreneurs hired fake black presidents to gain small business loans, (and even avant-garde magazines whose contributors are 95 percent white include blacks on their editorial boards in order to apply for multicultural grants), Hollywood has fielded fake producers like Oprah Winfrey and Tyler Perry and fake directors like Lee Daniels to face the flak that might rise from movies that blacks find objectionable. Steven Spielberg, who has produced two movies featuring black misogynists, but none about how members of his ethnic group treat women, followed this strategy.

For *The Help*, a black actress was used to defend the movie. Another sales decision of the white men who sponsor this junk, perhaps the same executives, who warn the hip-hoppers that their products will only be promoted if the lyrics are stupid, vile and nasty, is to spin that the only objections to this merchandise come from uptight disgruntled and bitter black men. Because I criticized Steven Spielberg's *The Color Purple*, white feminists and their black surrogates have carried on a relentless campaign against me. In the 1940s, another powerful special interest group damaged the careers of

Chester Himes and Richard Wright in the United States, yet just as the most severe criticism of *The Help* came from a group of black academic women, the strongest criticism of *The Color Purple* came from Nobel Laureate Toni Morrison. The same thing happened with *Precious*.

The only objection came from a few black male writers and news-men, so the spin went. In my interview with Terry McMillan, she has some of the same objections to the film as the men. She was one of those black women who also objected to Kathryn Stockett's *The Help*, one of whose actresses received an Oscar for playing yet another maid. But black women who write about the problems faced by even young middle class black men, when confronted by an American criminal justice system which tolerates torture, involun-tary experimentation with drugs, disparity in sentencing, and racial profiling, are ignored. This is why Adrienne Kennedy, on the short-list of great American playwrights, hasn't received a Pulitzer Prize, while the Pulitzer committee has rewarded a steady stream of black boogeyman books and theater. Her play, *Sleep Deprivation Chamber*, is a profound theatrical effort which shows the ordeal that not only young black inner city men must face in dealings with the police, but also young black men of the black middle class. This complex play with depth foreshadows the Trayvon Martin murder, one that has aroused the most mass demonstrations since the murder of Emmett Till. Broadway shuns Adrienne Kennedy's play that she co-wrote with her son Adam because it isn't black boogeyman enough to create a lucrative box office. It lacks the sales appeal of the revisionist *Porgy and Bess*, in which the role of Crown was recreated as that of a rapist instead of a seducer, borrowing from the very suc-cessful Willie Horton campaign, which was designed by Larry McCarthy.

So despite the fact that a few black women writers are being lion-ized, the middlemen, those who are just as good but who avoid the best-seller formula of producing books in which too-good-to-be-true women are surrounded by grunting beasts, are ignored, as are their opinions. Or dismissed, like Nafissatou Diallo, the hotel maid who said that she was forced into a non-consensual relationship with Strauss-Kahn. As an example of how the one percent who own the media rally around a one percenter who finds himself in a jam, the press, led by *The New York Times*, probed the victim's background looking for dirt that would discredit her. Dominique Strauss-Kahn, a former candidate vying to be president of France, was portrayed as someone who likes the arts. The *Times* tagged along as he dined in expensive restaurants and provided him with favorable coverage in 2011 on July 1, 26, and 30. *The New York Post* called the accuser a "hooker," (3 July 2011), while a French woman who made a similar claim against Strauss-Kahn was dismissed as a slut. The district attorney was called on the carpet for what was regarded by the media friends of the one percent as an overzealous prosecution. Yet what was the position of media feminist Chrystia Freeland, writing in *The Globe and Mail* on May 19, 2011? "But it is a grave and danger-ous mistake, with particularly baleful consequences for women, to argue that his history as a seducer, including in the workplace, makes him a more plausible offender. Yet that is what many are doing in the stunned aftermath of his arrest. The loudest culprits are an unlikely alliance of triumphant Anglo-Saxon puritans, feminists and the tabloid wing of the press. All are drawing a connecting line between his documented promiscuity and the allegation that he attempted rape and committed sexual assault last Saturday."

Like Arianna Huffington sold Shirley Sherrod, her black sister, down the river, Chrystia Freeland did the same to Nafissatou Diallo, whose name she didn't even mention in her column.

Jump to April 11, 2012 and we learn that "Residents were surprised over accusations that a prostitution ring tied to Dominique Strauss-Kahn operated out of the Hôtel Carlton de Lille." We also learned from columnist Joe Nocera on April 30, 2012 that "The day before the alleged assault…, Strauss-Kahn had participated in a sex party in Washington. He then flew to New York and got a room at the Sofitel, whose parent company employed an executive close to Sarkozy's intelligence coordinator, according to [Edward Jay] Epstein. After dinner, D.S.K. returned to the hotel with a woman who was seen exiting the ground-floor elevator at 3:56 a.m." The charge that black women are hankering to get into bed with white men is part of a historical pattern. I cover this in my essay, "She Wanted It..."

Ricky Taylor, whose gang rape by white men inspired the modern day Civil Rights Movement, didn't receive justice in her case but maybe Nafissatou Diallo, the housekeeper at the Sofitel in midtown Manhattan, will. A judge has rejected Dominique Strauss-Kahn's claim of diplomatic immunity in his effort to dismiss a civil suit filed by Nafissatou Diallo. Danielle L. McGuire, author of *At the Dark End of the Street: Black Women, Rape, and Resistance--A New History of the Civil Rights Movement from Rosa Parks to the Rise of Black Power*, appearing on C-Span, said that white women were silent as black women were raped by white men in the South. Is Ms. Freeland like those white women who ignored the situation of their black sisters who were assaulted by white men? Appearing on an edition of Howard Kurtz's *Reliable Sources*, which became a tribute to Strauss-Kahn, featuring a close friend of Strauss-Kahn, but absent any advocate for Nafissatou Diallo, Freeland went along with the patriarchs in dissing the hotel maid. Here's another example of how the opinions of minority women, black, Hispanic, Native American and Asian American women, are ignored. I've received so many tributes from minority and white women, some of which appear in a tribute published by Dave Eggers's McSweeny's publishing company, that I get embarrassed, but because two or three black women, surrogates for white female editors and white male publishers, who are silent about the abuses that women of their ethnic group suffer, have cast me as a misogynist, it's become my middle name.

The career of actor Lou Gossett shows what happens to an African-American artist who defies the trend that casts African Americans as rapists, maids who seduce powerful world leaders then lie about the encounter, thugs, sidekicks, entitlement dependents, and sub humans with low IQs. That is the position of *The New Republic, Commentary Magazine* and the Manhattan Institute, staffed by assimilated ex-white ethnics at whose ancestors the same libels were aimed by anti-Semites like novelist Henry James.

One of those who has consistently refused demeaning roles has been Lou Gossett. In my interview with Gossett the award-winning actor talks about what happens to you when you're both black and difficult in Hollywood. Another artist who has a reputation for being black and difficult is David Murray, the internationally known musician and composer. He talks about how he escaped the dependency on middlepersons and management. He follows in the footsteps of cultural entrepreneurs like W.C. Handy, who established his own music publishing company.

Just as subtle and harsh methods have been used to expel blacks from American cities—in New York, it was Mayor Giuliani and Mayor Michael Bloomberg's Gestapo "stop and frisk" measures that drove blacks from New York—ethnic cleansing has also occurred in the arts. David Murray observes that very few black jazz musicians are invited to European jazz festivals anymore and Ronnie Stewart of the Bay Area Blues Society says that the same thing is happening at blues festivals. Something similar is happening in literature. Nothing new. Langston Hughes complained that white playwrights wrote most of the plays about black life during his time. Richard Wright couldn't understand why black actors during the New Deal Works Progress Administration (WPA) period had to perform plays written by whites when there were plenty of black-written scripts available. I was invited to submit an outline for my memoirs by a major publishing house. It was concluded that a book of mine would only draw critical praise and awards. Instead, a book by a young white writer who referred to himself as an "angry black" was published. Like Richard Price and Eminem he had swapped his ethnic heritage for a black identity, just as Joel Chandler Harris and the white minstrels had done. Just as Ralph Ellison fumed because his friend William Styron had received more money writing about black life than he, black women writers are accusing Kathryn Stockett of invading their territory. I find that white writers have less success writing fiction about black life than non-fiction. When asked to name twenty of my favorite books, I realized that white authors wrote about a third and they were non-fiction.

Benjamin Drew in the title of his book, *A North-Side View of Slavery. The Refugee: or the Narratives of Fugitive Slaves in Canada* (Benjamin Drew 1812-1903), added, "as related by themselves." Maybe the condition of the black writer or interviewee of those days is similar to that of the writers of today. White audiences toward whom the media, Hollywood, and theater direct theater, prefer a version of black life that is toned down or packed with stereotypes with which they are comfortable, which in the case of *The Color Purple* and *Precious* they crave like an addict hungers for a fix.

My magazine *Konch*, has consistently published primary sources wherever possible instead of go-betweens. African writers write about Africa, Hispanic writers write about Hispanics. In the media, white men who dominate the public discussion are expected to be omniscient. To assume all points of view. It was the late Tim Russert who said that Thomas Friedman knew the Arab soul. Friedman recommends Victor David Hansen, a right-wing historian, as someone to consult about the Middle East. When I toured the Middle East, I was able to tell Arab journalists that I was one of the few publishers to print the views of Arab, Arab-American and Muslim intellectuals.

So what is a poet doing writing non-fiction about politics and culture? I wouldn't be the first. I refer to poet Lawrence Ferlinghetti's take down of President Eisenhower, who wanted the Supreme Court to uphold *Plessy v. Ferguson* and threatened China with nuclear warfare because for him life meant little to Asians. He wrote about the sinister and devious side of Eisenhower during a time when Eisenhower was hailed as an American Caesar in the 1950s, who'd returned victorious from foreign wars. Maybe a poet can spot information that eludes the academic or the pundit. For years, historians and commentators have traced the beginning of the Republican Southern strategy to Richard Nixon and Lee Atwater. I found an obscure speech by Harry Truman where he traces it to Eisenhower, viewed now as some kind of progressive because his farewell speech mentions "the military-industrial complex." The speech was written by Emmett Hughes. The president only read it.

Finally, while to millions in the world the United States looked as though it belonged in a straight jacket as insanity arose over the election of a black president, once again, our artists, whose dance, music, paintings, films and writings are admired throughout the world, gave a different exhibit as scores of artists carried the light from Robert Wilson's Watermill to many parts of the world, showing that in our country there was a glimmer of hope that we would survive this bad bad crazy season.

---

* Reports on the continued use of blacks and poor people as guinea pigs.

1) "California's Behavior Modification Programs –Abuse of Prisoners, Racism and Cover-Ups

"Ill-conceived experiments in behavior modification by the California Department of Corrections and Rehabilitation (CDCR) have led to allegations of racism, abuse of prisoners, retaliation and cover-ups, plus a state Senate inquiry.

"In 2005 and 2006, the CDCR initiated pilot programs in behavior modification at six facilities, including the High Desert State Prison (HDSP) in Susanville.

"Behavior modification is linked to a school of psychological thought which holds that a person's behavior can be influenced by application of appropriately timed rewards and punishments. It is derived primarily from the early 20th century work of Russian psychologist Ivan Pavlov, and was later popularized by American psychologist B.F. Skinner. In behavior therapy, emotional problems are considered the consequences of faulty acquired behavior patterns or the failure to learn effective responses. The aim of behavior therapy, therefore, is to change negative behavior patterns.

"There is little or no concern for unconscious processes (i.e., thoughts and feelings), which is the traditional focus of psychoanalysis, nor is there concern about achieving new insights or effecting fundamental personality changes.

In the Skinnerian approach, being rewarded while those that are not desired are punished reinforces desired behavioral responses. According to the theory, the frequency of rewarded behavior will increase; conversely, the frequency of behavior that is punished will decrease.

"Using such techniques, Skinner was able to train laboratory animals to perform complex and sometimes amazing acts—in one striking example, he taught pigeons to play table tennis. Subsequent researchers employed electric shocks to condition animals to experience fear in situations that ordinarily would not have provoked anxiety…." *Prisonlegalnews.org*

2) "Government-funded researchers tested AIDS drugs on hundreds of foster children over the past two decades, often without providing them a basic protection afforded in federal law and required by some states, an Associated Press review has found. The research funded by the National Institutes of Health spanned the country. It was most widespread in the 1990s as foster care agencies sought treatments for their HIV-infected children that weren't yet available in the marketplace." CBSNews.com:

3) "The Kennedy Krieger Institute in Baltimore was accused of knowingly exposing black children as young as a year old to lead poisoning in the 1990s." Timothy Williams, *The New York Times*, September 16, 2011.

4) "In *The Origins of AIDS*, Dr. Jacques Pépin starts from 1900 to work out the most likely path the virus took during the years it left almost no tracks. (Dr. Pépin says that he might have "inadvertently" injected African patients with AIDs virus as a result of dirty needles." Donald G. McNeil, Jr. *The New York Times*, October 18, 2011.

5) "Powerful drugs intended for people with severe mental illness are prescribed for children in foster care at a disturbingly high rate." Benedict Carey, *The New York Times*, November 21, 2011.

6) "Patients in state-run homes for the developmentally disabled have been receiving high doses of antipsychotics for behavior control, critics say, and the state is taking steps toward change." Danny Hakim, *The New York Times, N.Y./ Region*, December 23, 2011.

PART 1

Chief Executive and Chief Exorcist, Too?

President Obama
and the New Secession[1]

"As the first African-American president he's been up against a racist white bloc in the Republican Party that has come dressed as the Tea Party." Frank Schaeffer, author of *Sex, Mom & God*, interviewed by Jonathan Capehart, substituting for Martin Bashir on MSNBC, August 12, 2011

The Tea Party Congressmen and Congresswomen didn't go to Washington to insist upon fiscal responsibility, but to destroy the first black president. This is a racist movement in which holocaust deniers, Neo-Nazis and Neo-Confederates play a prominent role and whose members are drawn largely from the secessionist states, states that cited their desire to continue using human beings as property as the reason for their secession. Writing in *Salon.com* (20 August 2011) Michael Lind found that the majority of Tea Partiers are white men from the South. It figures, because the Tea Party is a secessionist movement and the filibustering against President Obama's programs, the most frequent use of the filibuster in history, amounts to a new nullification. Early on, Senator Mitch McConnell announced that his goal was to deny President Obama a second term. He's from Kentucky and though Kentucky was not part of the Confederacy, a Confederate "shadow government" was a powerful influence on the state government during the rebellion launched by traitors.

---

1. A version of this essay appeared at in *Black Renaissance/Renaissance Noire* in July 2011.

The Tea Party is founded on a racist Big Lie. Broker, Rick Santelli, who calls himself the Tea Party's "lightning rod," said that whites are angry because minorities are receiving all of the entitlements, when it would take a few hundred years for blacks and Hispanics to achieve the kind of government largess that has been accorded whites, which includes forced land grabs at the expense of blacks, Native Americans and Mexicans; the resistance to minorities gaining financial opportunities, from the driving out of the Chinese from gold mines to the racist policies of the Federal Housing Administration, which denied millions of blacks mortgages for decades. Whites also benefited from FDR programs (the G.I. Bill was called the "white" G.I. Bill), the Great Society programs, Medicaid, Medicare, Social Security, and federal highway programs that built their routes to the suburbs—suburbs that excluded blacks often by mob violence—just to mention a few. Whites even benefit from programs that were set up for the benefit of blacks like Affirmative Action. This is why there's a sixty percent enrollment of white women in colleges and universities. In ten years, it will be seventy percent. This is not the only program that's supposed to benefit blacks but ends up benefiting whites. Take the Small Business Administration. Associated Press reported on April 17, 1994 that "Minority Programs Mostly Aid Whites. The government's flagship program for minority entrepreneurs awarded $19 billion in contracts over the last six years, with the lion's share going to firms whose headquarters were located in primarily white, well-to-do neighborhoods. An Associated Press computer analysis of 'minority set-aside' contracts handled by the Small Business Administration found that 22 percent of the project dollars went to companies located in minority areas." The highest form of hypocrisy is exposed when one finds that Santelli's Tea Party, those who are offended by minorities benefiting from entitlements, are hogging all of the welfare. In an article entitled "Moochers Against Welfare," Paul Krugman ridicules Moochers Against Welfare, published in *The New York Times*, February 16, 2012

> Now, there's no mystery about red-state reliance on government programs. These states are relatively poor, which means both that people

have fewer sources of income other than safety-net programs and that more of them qualify for "means-tested" programs such as Medicaid.

By the way, the same logic explains why there has been a jump in dependency since 2008. Contrary to what Mr. Santorum and Mr. Romney suggest, Mr. Obama has not radically expanded the safety net. Rather, the dire state of the economy has reduced incomes and made more people eligible for benefits, especially unemployment benefits. Basically, the safety net is the same, but more people are falling into it.

But why do regions that rely on the safety net elect politicians who want to tear it down? I've seen three main explanations.

First, there is Thomas Frank's thesis in his book *What's the Matter With Kansas?*: working-class Americans are induced to vote against their own interests by the G.O.P.'s exploitation of social issues. And it's true that, for example, Americans who regularly attend church are much more likely to vote Republican, at any given level of income, than those who don't.

One could say that in comparison to blacks, Native Americans, Hispanics and South Asians, the white middle class is living in a social-ist utopia, however the upper class whites, with whom they formed an alliance under the banner of a Reaganite white nationalism, might be ready to jettison them. Jewish Americans who thought they'd been accepted into this coalition are now being threatened by the far right, which the Tea Party represents. This movement is anti-Semitic as well as racist. Maybe those Jewish Neo-Cons at *The New Republic* and *Commentary* (whose black representative is John McWhorter), who felt so secure in the embrace of white nationalism that they supported quack theories about black intellectual inferiority, will notice this new threat to the security of Jewish Americans. David Frum and David Brooks, who are urging the Republicans to cultivate white students and the white working class, should spend a year in Georgia, Mississippi, and South Carolina. Test their whiteness.

Despite Manhattan Institute spokesperson John McWhorter's claim that racial profiling is the last issue facing blacks, millions of blacks have been denied the kind of advantages accorded whites when buying homes. (McWhorter's changed his mind since he was used by *Commentary* to dismiss racial profiling as an issue; after the Trayvon Martin murder, McWhorter and other post-racers have retreated from this position, since Martin was the poster boy for the post generation; he enjoyed horseback riding and skiing. After denouncing my book *Another Day At The Front*, McWhorter just about admitted that he was wrong.) As late as Sunday, July 31, 2011, Tom Brokaw was blaming the economic crisis on minorities who bought homes that they couldn't afford. MSNBC's black correspondent Jonathan Capehart agreed. The reason that millions of whites regard blacks as failures, as drug addicts, as Affirmative Action babies, is because they get most of their information about blacks from news correspondents, Hollywood and politicians who embrace the same stereotypes about black Americans as they. Though some of the black commentators have some verve, the opinions of others are managed by white producers who demand that they be even handed so that they won't alienate their white consumers. This is why Melissa Harris-Perry had to say that "there are a lot of things that she likes about the Tea Party." What things? People showing up at the president's rallies armed? Ugly signs like those of the president as a witchdoctor or lying in a coffin? Prominent Tea Party members calling for his assassination or insisting that he was born in Kenya?

The propaganda promoted by Santini and others that blacks receive entitlements more than others is a false claim. So is the one about blacks getting into trouble for taking out mortgages that they couldn't afford. It fails to recognize that the banks discriminated against blacks by leading them to loans that bore higher interest rates, yet it fits the Tea Party's argument. Even *The Wall Street Journal* notes that sixty percent of blacks and Hispanics were eligible for conventional loans, but were denied because of the racist practices of the mortgage industry, details of which were developed in an article by Tanya Dennis, "Banking While Black," *Oakland Post* (3-9 August 2011). Moreover, the state with the highest number of foreclosures was Nevada, a state with a small black population.

Paul Krugman, columnist for *The New York Times*, is among the economists who've challenged this suburban myth. (This is the

Krugman who is treated as the leading economist of the white power shadow government; he's had it in for Obama since the campaign when he called Obama supporters "a cult." Another critic is Frank Rich, the Don Imus supporter who now works at *New York* magazine. Constantly quoted by Obama detractors, Rich has called Obama "slippery".)

And so the Tea Party, financed by some of the 2 percent—mostly oil companies whom Barack Obama would make pay taxes and whose subsidies he would end, is based upon lies, hypocrisy and most of all, racism. But left and liberal commentators are reluctant to classify them as such for fear of being accused of playing the race card. Such is the intimidation that the Tea Party uses against its adversaries that *The New York Times* columnist Joe Nocera had to apologize to the Tea Partiers for calling them "terrorists." Standard & Poor's, the credit rating agency, cited Republican (Tea Party) intransigence five times on page 4 of its report as its reason for lowering the United States' credit rating from triple A to double A plus, yet the line promoted by CNN on Sunday August 7 and MSNBC, August 8, was that all were at fault.

The next day, while casting blame for the downgrading of United States' credit, CNN showed a huge picture of President Obama. (I was watching this CNN report while standing in line at the Kaiser pharmacy in Oakland.) Next to the picture of Obama, representing the executive department, was a picture of the Capitol building, but no photos of Grover Norquist, House Majority Leader Eric Cantor from Virginia, or Republican Speaker of the House from Ohio, John Boehner, as though the only human responsible for the crisis was the president. (An elderly white woman who was in line behind me said, "Why don't they leave him (Obama) alone?" A middle aged white man standing in front of me agreed with her that CNN was ambushing Obama.) John Chambers, head of Standard and Poor's Sovereign Rating Committee, blamed the downgrading on Congress's inability to raise the debt ceiling in a timely manner, yet the head mooner of the Tea Party, Michelle Bachmann, also blamed the financial crisis on Obama.

The white males, who still monopolize the airwaves and opinion pages, progressive, liberal, left and right, exclude the discussion of race when discussing the Tea Party. One of the reasons is because the producers, who are fond of making racist comments in private, are reluctant to turn off their angry white male customers with discussions of race. This applies to the progressive as well as the mainstream media. The progressives, to the consternation of the blacks among them, still rank class above race, historically. They still long for the day when the white working class will join ranks with blacks, Hispanics and other minorities and rise up against the Bosses, their version of the apocalypse. A mirage. This is why some progressives advocate an alliance with the Tea Party which they view as a working class uprising against Wall Street when the Tea Party in Congress was sent there to prevent liberals and progressives from taxing Wall Street and ending oil subsidies, which is why millions of dollars in Texas oil money are behind these pitiful saps.

W.E.B. Du Bois and Booker T. Washington might have had disagreements, but they both commented about the racism of the white working class. Progressives have been accused of "white chauvinism" by black progressives since the 1920s. They still believe that it's all about class and not race even though the white workers have spurned most attempts to join in a coalition with minorities, sometimes by using violence.

The reason that the left is now led by white men who lack street smarts and are prone to this kind of naivety is because the white middle class feminist movement, which has gained influence over left wing politics, pushed black men to the margins of the movement by casting them as symbols of male misogyny. Even heroes like Malcolm X and Martin Luther King, Jr. are now being subjected to what amounts to misogyny show trials, in the press and on Broadway, as a result of entertainment financed by white men. In an earlier period, it was W.E.B. Du Bois and Booker T. Washington who were subject to ridicule: Du Bois for his radical politics, Washington, after dining with Theodore Roosevelt and after being beaten in New York.

Contrast the attitudes of Du Bois and Washington toward the white working class with that of Congressman Bernie Sanders, who wanted to primary Obama. He describes the Tea Party as one that reflects the frustrations of working class people. He must be crazy. Appearing on *The Chris Matthews Show*, just as clueless, on August 2, 2011, "progressive" Congressman Barney Frank said he didn't detect any racist leanings among the Tea Party members of Congress.

The Tea Party's racist roots weren't even mentioned by an all white male progressive panel on KPFA's *Sunday Salon* (31 July 2011) on which the vitriolic Obama bashing was led by Matthew Rothschild, the editor of *The Progressive*. This guy was allowed to go out on Obama, to lose his mind about Obama for nearly an hour. Not once did the white guests and moderator mention the racist appeals that were used to build the Tea Party. Not once! Bill Maher who thinks that he's so hip and outrageous had among his guests Matt Kibbe of Freedom Works (29 July 2011). Not once did Maher mention that Dick Armey's Freedom Works has received twelve million dollars from the Koch brothers.

Obama hater Gloria Borger of CNN commended the Tea Party as people who came to Washington to assert their principles; people who couldn't be bought by promises of earmarks. People who are not beholden to party leaders; this is because their bills are paid by people like the Koch brothers. They're beholden to the rich who sent them there. A group of blondes, one of whom was from England and another a descendant of Herbert Hoover, were brought on MSNBC to criticize the president. Among them was Michelle Cottle who saluted the Tea Party's "purity." She works for *The Daily Beast* whose publisher Tina Brown is a Palin supporter. On August 7, 2011, *The Daily Beast* printed the comments of PUMA's Leslie Bennetts, who urged a Hillary Clinton primary challenge against Obama.

Purity? This is a movement whose former presidential candidate Michele Bachmann and her family have received hundreds of thousands of dollars from government programs. Receiving government assistance for their farm, counseling service and mortgage. Tea Party members also believe that their morals are superior to those of minorities. *The Chicago Sun Times* revealed that one of their spokes-persons, Joe Walsh, Republican Congressman from Illinois, was a deadbeat dad. The Tea Party members say that the government should be run like a family, yet Taxpayers for Common Sense shows some of the Tea Party Congressmen to be heavily in debt. The media helped to create the Tea Party—in July 2011, CNN covered a Tea Party rally to which only 50 people showed up; the media covered a rally in St. Louis where only 3 showed up. So much so that one could term the Tea Party the media's brain child since Murdoch's Fox News, led by Willie Horton mastermind Roger Ailes, promoted the Tea Party while its call to arms was issued by Rick Santelli, who appeared on CNBC and delivered an ugly incoherent diatribe against the president: he launched the racist canard that whites were paying for foreclosures that resulted from blacks defaulting on their mortgages. The anti-Obama media can also be guilty of a conflict of interest.

Obama wants to raise the taxes for corporations like General Electric, which pays no taxes. General Electric has a large number of shares in NBC. You mean to tell me that this doesn't account for the hiring of black Republicans like Michael Steele and others to comment on the president's performance? Joe Scarborough gets to rant against Obama for three hours every morning. He even has Roger Welch on to criticize Obama. Welch is the former head of General Electric. For its part, CNN actually has hired former Bush and Cheney aides Frances M. Fragos Townsend, former Homeland Security advisor to U.S. President George W. Bush, and Mary Joe Matalin, former assistant to Dick Cheney until 2003, to judge Obama. As head of Simon & Shuster's Threshold Editions, she pub-lished the most scurrilous book about the president. It was called *Obama Nation* and was written by birther Jerome R. Corsi, the co-author of *Unfit for Command*, the book that libeled John Kerry. Both MSNBC and CNN use black commentators to represent the Republican Party, when George Bush only received two percent of the black vote and 90 of black voters voted for Obama, a Democrat.

CNN refuses to reveal the hundreds of millions behind the move-ment, describing a Tea Party that's like Jimmy Stewart who went to

Washington and stood up for his principles in the movie *Mr. Smith Goes to Washington*, rather than a group of mostly over-fifty white males who continue to vote against their interests, a phenomenon that continues to puzzle white progressives and liberals. Every black person with the possible exception of the black talking heads on TV knows why millions of white voters bond with millionaires and billionaires who only use the United States for a change of clothes before jetting off to another party in Monaco.

Obama's election was supposed to herald the arrival of a post-race America. Instead it has shown the depth of the American racial pathology, that some are so full of hatred for the president they are willing to destroy the world economy rather than see him re-elected. This hatred approaching psychosis recommends that the American Psychological Association reconsider the request of black psychologists that racism be considered a mental illness. That some powerful fanatics with only an 18 percent approval rating are able to threaten the world economy by holding the assets of millions hostage, is something that deserves a more precise scrutiny. As a result of their lunacy, all of us, including the Tea Party members, will be charged higher interest for home and auto loans and credit cards. Oh, right, there are black racists, but they are not as motivated as the white ones. During the twentieth century there wasn't one black Timothy McVeigh.

Though Obama still has the majority of Latino, black and white Democrats and liberals backing him, his black critics are provided with generous airtime and are immune from criticism. Nobody asks who pays for Obama critics Cornel West and Tavis Smiley's "poverty tour." On the first leg of their poverty tour they were greeted by angry black Detroiters who were opposed to their tour. And why hasn't Tavis Smiley been required to explain his ties to Wells Fargo, a bank that has had to pay fines for arranging illegal mortgage loans with blacks?

Though millions of whites voted for the first black president, some of those in the top two percent, who have thrived since the 1800s by pitting blacks against whites, were back in business. They put their bucks into recruiting an army of resentful fatuous pathetic serfs, entitlements dependents who are opposed to entitlements, whom the rich ridicule in private. Their job is to do the dirty work of overturning the will of the electorate. The army's philosopher is Grover Norquist, who is a front man for moneyed interests including Time Warner, which explains why CNN, a Time Warner subsidiary, has been so supportive of the Tea Party under the claim of "objectivity."

It explains why CNN inflates the numbers of those who attend Tea Party rallies, while ignoring demonstrations for left causes that draw hundreds of thousands. Grover Norquist wants to save his sponsors from paying taxes by strangling government. In the past, he supported South Africa's apartheid regime. He called President Obama "prissy," repeatedly. Prissy? President Obama and his family receive death threats daily, racist taunts on network television, armed men attending his rallies, which is one of the reasons General Colin Powell, a five star general refused to run. Prissy? Obama's ordering the capture of Osama bin Laden has been described as one of the gutsiest decisions made by a recent American president. Moreover, why hasn't the gay community, including the gay con- servative organization, GOProud, condemned Norquist for using a homophobic slur in describing the president? Shouldn't GOProud dismiss Norquist as a member of its advisory council? (see www. goproud.org).

Should Obama run again? If he were to serve one term he'd be ranked as a superior president by future historians. He saved the nation from a depression and destroyed Al-Qaeda by taking out bin Laden, erased Don't Ask, Don't Tell. These are only a few of his accomplishments. Running again will increase the possibility of a "lone-gunman-who-only-paranoids-would-believe-was-part-of-a-conspiracy" doing harm to him, or members of his family. He can probably contribute more by using his prestige as an ex-president like Carter and Clinton.

A second term will only lead to more grey hairs, sleepless nights, anxiety and could possibly lead him to start smoking again, which will further destroy his organs and precipitate lung cancer. We lost

Malcolm, Martin Luther King Jr., RFK, and JFK who were in their prime. We need one of ours to stay around for a while.

If he runs again he will be pestered by progressives who represent only a fraction of the Democratic Party but who get generous media time because they are anti-Obama. (They continue to believe naively that the Tea Party is a grass roots uprising against Wall Street.) Some of the worst bad mouthing of Obama comes from "progressive" sites like *Salon.com*, *Firedog Lake*, and *The Nation*. Katrina Vanden Heuvel, *The Nation*'s editor wouldn't even give credit to Obama for capturing bin Laden. *The Nation*'s John Nichols says that Obama is shameful. *Nation* contributor Ari Melber has been especially critical, whiny, petty and abusive. He said that all that Obama had accomplished was modest health care reform and Don't Ask Don't Tell. Tell that to the millions of autoworkers whose jobs were saved because Obama bailed out the auto industry and the estimated two to three million who held jobs as a result of the stimulus. The "progressive" *Nation* beats up on Fox News, yet Fox has a higher percentage of black contributors than *The Nation*; the special sports issue, edited by radical sports commentator, David Zirin, didn't include one black or Latino contributor. Paul Krugman says that Obama should have spent more on the stimulus, ignoring the fact that the Republican Party blocked his wishes. He wanted to close Guantanamo. The Republicans blocked that. Progressive radio's Nicole Sandler says that Obama hasn't accomplished anything. Sonali Kolhatkar, host of a Pacifica show called *Uprising*, is a progressive who ridicules the president weekly. She says that all the president is good at is making speeches echoing the Republican Party's criticism of the president.

When I reminded white progressives that they weren't his base since the majority of Democrats still supported Obama, I got bawled out by *Salon*'s Joan Walsh, who called my comment, "pernicious." She said that she was resentful of my saying that blacks were his political base. I made no such comment and her readers reminded her, yet she still refuses to provide a link to my *New York Times* article where I criticized the vanity of white progressives. (See *Joan Walsh's Twitter Brawl with Herself*, p. 59.)

The badmouthing of the president led to the billionaire Koch brothers funded puppet Tea Party victory in 2010 because, influenced by the incitement of progressives, thousands of voters stayed home. Gays stayed home because they didn't get *Don't Ask Don't Tell* dropped fast enough. White women stayed home even though Obama, on January 29, 2009, signed the Lilly Ledbetter Fair Pay Act, which accords equal pay to women. The president put two women—Sonia Sotomayor in 2009 and Elena Kagan in 2010—on the Supreme Court. But despite these Obama driven accomplishments for women, a recent Pew poll says that the percentage of white women who wish to join the Republican Party has increased. Like the PUMAs at *The Daily Beast*, who want to ensure a Republican victory by urging that Obama be primaried, some women want to risk the election of those who would condemn them to back-alley abortions and return them to house arrest.

Some women are the last of the oppressed to vote for people who would deny them choice. This is nothing new. While visiting Montreal in 2010, I learned that in 1957 Southern white women had sponsored a plaque still on the front of a major department store because Jefferson Davis, who led an uprising against the federal government, had spent some nights there with a wealthy Englishman, despite the fact that the Confederacy was a feudal regime run by a Taliban type patriarchy that denied them power. Jefferson Davis's troops were within five minutes of firing on white women who participated in the Richmond bread riots in 1863. Los Angeles NOW even endorsed Arnold Schwarzenegger for governor, despite *The Los Angeles Times* having run an expose of his sexual aggression toward women. Obviously the middle class feminist movement has failed to educate their white sisters. They've been too busy supporting "black boogeyman" products and blaming misogyny on Kobe Bryant, Mike Tyson, Clarence Thomas and yes, Emmett Till.

But Obama's most rabid opposition will come from Congressional diehards who believe that if Stonewall Jackson had been in charge at Gettysburg instead of Robert E. Lee, we'd be living under a different system today. They will thwart Obama at every turn. If they elect Mitt Romney, Marie Antoinette in a business suit, and the Red States realize that those who are entitlement dependent are them, maybe we'll see some drastic change in this country, for better or worse.

Why Some White Progressives Make Me Sick[1]

R alph Ellison wrote his novel, *Invisible Man*, in an elliptical style because the House Un-American Activities Committee was breathing down the necks of black writers. Langston Hughes, appearing before the committee, had to renounce his left-leaning pro-Soviet poetry.

But stripped bare, Ellison's book is about the left's abandonment of the issue of housing foreclosures. Progressives of the day turned their attention to saving the communist revolution abroad, under attack by German fascists. Ellison was furious about what he considered a betrayal.

I thought about this switch in concerns when I recently received an email inviting me to participate in No Torture Week by a progressive Berkeley group. They meant torture at Abu Ghraib. Nothing about torture in Illinois, New York, New Mexico and California prisons, recently uncovered in an investigative report from *The Sacramento Bee*.

Amy Goodman found a case of torture in the Philippines, when torture is occurring at Riker's Island, not far from her firehouse studio. Ms. Goodman has become the progressive voice on CNN. Appearing there, she threatened President Obama that if he didn't

---

1. A version of this essay appeared at *Counterpunch.org*, September 17-19, 2010.

bring about universal health care, progressives would stay home during the upcoming election.

One of her guests was Eve Ensler, the creator of *The Vagina Monologues*. She is directing an all black women ensemble in a performance called *Swimming Upstream*, about the Katrina disaster as though black men were out of town when the flood occurred. Maybe partying in Las Vegas with Tiger Woods and Mike Tyson.

There doesn't seem to be any room for minority men in the world of this kind of feminist.

During her appearance on *Democracy Now*, Ms. Ensler was right to denounce the rape of Congo women by soldiers, but she spent only a fraction of her time on the multinational corporations that are financing "rebels" all over Africa and the arming of the soldiers by American firms. (That's not all that American firms are arming. Ninety percent of the weapons used by Mexican drug lords have an American source, and the illegal weapons are pouring into cities like mine from the suburbs.) As Hugh Masekela, the great South African trumpeter, told me during an interview, "All African wars are surrogate wars." Malian writer Manthia Diawara (*We Won't Budge*), chair of Africana Studies at NYU, says that whites still run Africa.

So blinded by her fury at black men in the Congo, Haiti and New Orleans, Ms. Ensler gave little attention to the manipulation of African wars by the misogynists operating behind the scenes. She said that what united the Congo, Haiti and New Orleans was rape. Even *The New York Times*, which runs mug shots of blacks everyday, while giving scant attention to corporate crime (hidden away in the Business section), exposed the fraudulent reporting that had widespread mayhem, rape and looting occurring during Katrina.

But at least Ms. Ensler didn't accuse the blacks of New Orleans of cannibalism. It took the progressive *Huffington Post* to float that lie, according to Robin Solit, a genuine progressive. The *Huffington Post* is run by Arianna Huffington, the multimillion-dollar progressive whose telegenic smile and accent gets her on a lot of shows. She's been Obama's bane. Calling upon Joe Biden to resign, a stunt that got her more airtime.

In the 1950s, I used to attend socialist meetings in Buffalo, New York. Once in a while Corliss Lamont (son of the chairman at J.P. Morgan) would address the meetings. He was a multimillionaire progressive like Ms. Huffington. The socialists would take his money but snicker at him behind his back. A multimillionaire progressive was considered a joke in those days.

The crime of rape is historically one of the most atrocious acts of war. It doesn't just happen in Africa, Haiti and New Orleans. Some of Ms. Ensler's comments smacked of Gyno Fascism. She said:

> And I began to understand that violence against women is central to everything. You know, if you're destroying the female population, if you're destroying your mother and your sister, you know, and your daughter, you're essentially destroying life itself. So, how do we as human beings continue on, if what is essential about life is being eviscerated and devastated?

Men aren't essential to life? British scientists have found a way to make human sperm from embryonic stem cells, but isn't it still a good idea to have men around?

Moreover, what about the millions of men who actually get murdered in these wars? I'm all for the emancipation of Iraqi and Iranian women, but what about millions of men who were killed in wars between Iraq and Iran—wars manipulated by the same crowd that is now fighting China over Africa's resources? Men who were killed by chemicals supplied by American firms.

What about the high male casualties that resulted from the Gulf War and the thousands who've been killed as a result of the American occupation of Iraq—an occupation that has resulted in rape and the kind of prostitution that has occurred wherever American troops have found themselves?

One of the reasons that the left is teetering is because of women like Ensler, who suggested during her interview that men are not as essential to life as women.

In the 1960s, The Nation of Islam promoted a myth that became a vogue in black intellectual and artistic circles (while the majority of working and middle class blacks remained Christians). It had white people created by a black scientist named Yacub. This Yacub character grafted whites from blacks and set them loose upon the world to do evil.

Even someone as hip and smart as Amiri Baraka wrote a Yacub play called *A Black Mass* (1966). At the end of the play, the newly created whites, played by black actors in whiteface, leap from the stage and, foaming at the mouth, begin to attack members of the audience. When Wallace D. Muhammad succeeded his father, Elijah Muhammad, he, an orthodox Muslim, abandoned Yacubism. Baraka abandoned the idea in the 70s and became a Communist. The man responsible for popularizing the myth, Elijah Muhammad, never really believed it. In connection with my new book, *The Fighter and the Writer*, I've discovered that Elijah Muhammad entertained whites at his dinner table.

A sort of gender Yacubism is operating in white and black feminist circles, but instead of evil whites being created by a scientist, it's evil men.

Just as a movement that demonized whites failed, a movement that favors one gender over another is a loser and as a result the power of black men on the left has been diminished. Unfortunate, because they once were a potent force on the left.

While Ms. Ensler's *Swimming Upstream* was made available in large spaces, including the New Orleans Superdome and Harlem's Apollo Theater, there is little space in the progressive branch of the Jim Crow media available for the testimony of New Orleans black writers like Mona Lisa Saloy, Kalamu ya Salaam, and Jerry Ward (his classic is *The Katrina Diaries*), writers who actually survived Katrina. They don't get on CNN or *Democracy Now*, or *Air America*. We need Eve Ensler, David Simon and Harry Connick, Jr., and Dr. John, the singer who covers the legendary Professor Longhair, to tell us what it was like.

While Goodman progressives long for the kind of homophobic dictatorship that now runs Cuba, *Nation* magazine progressives want another Roosevelt.

Appearing on Ms. Goodman's show, *The Nation*'s John Nichols suggested that President Obama make a Roosevelt-style speech about Us, the masses of people, against Them, the moneyed interests. What Mr. Nichols doesn't understand is that millions of whites identify with the Them. Why else would they join faux populist groups bankrolled by billionaires who get them drunk on the cheap draft beer of white supremacy. (Carrying racist signs. One of them showed Barack Obama lying in a coffin. I couldn't believe it! I put the TV set on pause and took a picture of it.) These Tea Partiers are loyal to the fourteen thousand families who own one quarter of the country's wealth as long as members of the one percent use their media to flatter them at the expense of scapegoats, blacks, Hispanics, and Muslims. The mental illness of white supremacy, an infectious super bug, is evident when you consider that the young black president, who is hated by these media-coached, rabid, howling mobs, saved them from a depression. The majority of economists agree about that.

Moreover, the status of whites was different in Roosevelt's time. Nichols ought to read the fiction of Jack Conroy, or Tillie Olsen, proletarian writers who wrote about the millions of whites whose 1930s existence was one of desperation. Read William Kennedy's *Ironweed*. Though white poverty still exists (check the *Jerry Springer Show* any day or the films of Debra Granik), millions of whites, after entering the middle class, became Reagan Democrats. Where once there were Italian Americans, Irish Americans, Jewish Americans, there are now "whites." Some of those who had forged alliances with blacks went uptown on them. Started playing the harpsichord. Started giving money to the Metropolitan Museum. Some Irish Americans began publishing a magazine called *The National Review*, which supported quack Kantian anthropology about African inferiority. Ironic because early Nativists didn't want the Irish to come here because they said that the Irish had a "crime gene."

How did Roosevelt feel about black unemployment? He made a deal with the Dixiecrats that excluded blacks from receiving some benefits of the New Deal. (See: *When Affirmative Action was White:*

An Untold History of Racial Inequality in Twentieth Century America by Ira Katznelson.)

Robert Scheer, interviewed on Berkeley's KPFA by Kris Welch, is another example of a progressive who hasn't a clue about the situation of blacks and Hispanics.

During his critique of the banking policies that led to a near depression, he longed for a mythical Mr. Pillsbury, the neighborhood banker who used to hand out mortgage loans to qualified borrowers like candy. That might have been true for white borrowers, but whether Mr. Scheer knows it or not, there was rarely a Mr. Pillsbury for black and Hispanic borrowers as a result of the historic racist practices of the mortgage industry. These racist practices and those of the FHA have placed blacks in the position where their savings have been used to finance white businesses and home ownership. Since Reconstruction! That's got to add up to trillions of dollars. A sort of reverse reparations! Denied access to capital, they become renters who help white investors pay off the mortgages incurred by their investment properties. They are denied the chance to develop equity. They can't take advantage of the sixty-year-old tax deduction for interest on mortgages, a white entitlement program. And these people who listen to people like Goebbels I, Rupert Murdoch, and his Beelzebub assistant, Roger Ailes, believe that blacks are getting all of the entitlements?

Scheer seemed to blame those whom he referred to as "minorities, the poor and drug addicts" for the recession because of policies that opened the mortgage-lending market to people like these who couldn't afford to pay. He agrees with billionaire Antoinettist, Thomas Friedman, who came to the same conclusion, a conclusion disputed by Friedman's *Times* colleague Paul Krugman. On June 14, 2010, Peter Hart cited a Tom Friedman column of the day before in which the columnist blamed the housing bubble on selling houses to poor people. "We–both parties–created massive tax incentives and cheap money to make home mortgages available to people who really didn't have the means to sustain them." (Friedman's colleague Ross Douthat, the *Times*' idea of a conservative, says that there is "white anxiety" over Affirmative Action, prompting yet another letter from Julian Bond reminding him that Affirmative Action is a white program and benefits whites the most.)

Moreover even *The Wall Street Journal* reports that over sixty percent of those who received subprime loans were eligible for conventional loans. Why didn't they receive them? Something that Scheer overlooked. Recent studies from Brandeis University and the Center for Responsible Lending offer clues: According to the study by the Institute on Assets and Social Policy at Brandeis University, the wealth gap between African-American families and white families has jumped dramatically in 23 years. In fact, the difference in financial assets between these two groups has increased over four times in a generation, from $20,000 in 1984 to $95,000 in 2007.

The Brandeis report also found that middle-income whites experienced a greater increase in net worth than high-income blacks. Average white families earning $30,000 had accumulated $74,000, while blacks earning more than $50,000 owned only $18,000, for a wealth gap of $56,000.

To make things worse, ten percent of African-Americans owed at least $3,600, nearly doubling their debt burden since 1984. And sadly, at least a quarter of black families had no assets to rely upon for when times get rough.

So, what's the problem here? The problem is that income equality is not translating into wealth equality and economic security for black households. Some of this is due to bad public policy, including tax breaks for the wealthiest Americans, and other measures that have redistributed wealth upwards—to those who are already rich and arguably don't need more.

But there is another reason, namely, institutional racism in housing, labor and lending. The deregulation of the lending market has resulted in systemic discrimination against people of color and the poor, who pay more for credit. Those who live paycheck to paycheck borrow just to make ends meet, depending increasingly on payday lending, a.k.a. legal loan sharks, and check-cashing stores that prey on these poorer communities. Blacks and Latinos have been steered into risky, costly and sketchy subprime mortgages, at more than twice the rate of whites with the same income. The foreclosure crisis has wiped out what little wealth many of these families owned, placing a stranglehold on the ability of the African-American community to build wealth.

Similarly, according to another report, communities of color were disproportionately cut out of conventional mortgage loans after the housing bubble burst.

Progressives have been telling blacks that class not race determines status in American society at least since the 1920s when Mike Gold of the Communist Party and poet Claude McKay had a falling out over the issue. But when it comes to the racist and corrupt mortgage industry, this isn't true. Whites with lower credit ratings receive better loans than blacks with high credit ratings.

This from the Center for Responsible Lending:

> It is well documented that African-American and Latino families disproportionately received the most expensive and dangerous types of loans during the heyday of the subprime market. According to analyses of the Home Mortgage Disclosure Act data, higher-rate conventional mortgages were disproportionately distributed to borrowers of color between 2004 and 2008. For example, in 2006, among consumers who received conventional mortgages for single-family homes, roughly half of African-American (53.7 percent) and Hispanic borrowers (46.5 percent) received a higher-rate mortgage compared to about one-fifth of non-Hispanic white borrowers (17.7 percent). In addition, a Center for Responsible Learning study showed that African-American and Latino borrowers were more likely to receive higher-rate subprime loans than white borrowers with similar risk profiles, while another study provided evidence that loans in minority communities were more likely to carry prepayment penalties than loans in white communities, even after controlling for other factors. It therefore stands to reason that borrowers of color, which were targeted by sub prime lenders and steered into the most abusive products, would be disproportionately bearing the brunt of this foreclosure crisis.

Minorities, the poor, and drug addicts taking out mortgages that they couldn't afford to pay, Mr. Scheer?

While some progressives believe that class is, using multi-millionaire Gloria Steinem's phrase, "the most restrictive factor in American life," feminists, genderists, and others believe that it's sexual orientation.

After my essay on *Precious* appeared in *The New York Times* (See "Fade to White", p. 117) I got letters from white gays arguing that blacks and gays share a similar history or in a couple of cases that gays have been more restricted in American life than blacks. Who do you think had a better chance of receiving bank loans in San Francisco, which is now regentrified? Blacks or gays?

(Rick Santelli, appearing on Chris Matthews, exploded a loud fib when he implied that minorities get all of the entitlements, a propaganda line that Ronald Reagan performed. Santelli, who calls himself "the lightning rod" for the Tea Party movement, says that this is what galvanizes the Tea Partiers, people who have helped themselves to government programs: FDR's, the Great Society, the War On Poverty, Medicare, Social Security, the G.I. Bill, etc.)

While Scheer went off on President Obama about his polices, other progressives are annoyed with his style. David Corn says that Obama should put more passion into his speeches, but Corn said he liked Obama's critique of the black family. He is one of those who believes that fatherless homes is a black problem, exclusively, in a country where fifty percent of marriages end in divorce and the nuclear family comes in at about five percent. As someone who has lived in the inner city for thirty years and grew up in one, I can assure you that there is a man in these homes.

As the late playwright August Wilson said, "On the weekends, the parking lots in the projects are full."

What Progressives Don't Understand About Obama[1]

Not all of my white teachers viewed me as a discipline problem. To the annoyance of my fellow students, one teacher selected me regularly to lead assembly programs. A high school teacher insisted that I learn about the theater. She was an America-firster who supplied me with right-wing pamphlets and magazines that I'd read at breakfast and she didn't seem bothered by my returning them with some of the pages stuck together with syrup.

But most of them did see me as an annoyance, and gave me the grades to prove it.

I've been thinking recently of all those D's for deportment on my report cards. I thought of them, for instance, when I read a response to an essay I had written about Mark Twain that appeared in *A New Literary History of America*. One of the country's leading critics, who writes for a prominent progressive blog, called the essay "rowdy," which I interpreted to mean "lack of deportment." Perhaps this was because I cited *Huckleberry Finn* to show that some white women managed household slaves, a departure from the revisionist theory that sees Scarlett O'Hara as some kind of feminist martyr.

I thought of them when I pointed out to a leading progressive that the Tea Party included neo-Nazis and Holocaust deniers—and he called me a "bully." He believes that the Tea Party is a grass-roots uprising against Wall Street, a curious reading since the movement

1. A version of this essay appeared in *The New York Times* on December 11, 2010.

gained its impetus from a rant against the president delivered by a television personality on the floor of the Chicago Mercantile Exchange.

And I've thought about them as I've listened recently to progressives criticize President Obama for keeping his cool.

Progressives have been urging the president to "man up" in the face of the Republicans. Some want him to be like John Wayne. On horseback. Slapping people left and right.

One progressive commentator played an excerpt from a Harry Truman speech during which Truman screamed about the Republican Party to great applause. He recommended this style to Mr. Obama. If President Obama behaved that way, he'd be dismissed as an angry black militant with a deep hatred of white people. His grade would go from a B- to a D.

What the progressives forget is that black intellectuals have been called "paranoid," "bitter," "rowdy," "angry," "bullies," and accused of tirades and diatribes for more than one hundred years. Very few of them would have been given a grade above D from most of my teachers.

When these progressives refer to themselves as Mr. Obama's base, all they see is themselves. They ignore polls showing steadfast support for the president among blacks and Latinos. And now they are whispering about a primary challenge against the president. Brilliant! The kind of suicidal gesture that destroyed Jimmy Carter— and a way to lose the black vote forever.

Unlike white progressives, blacks and Latinos are not used to getting it all. They know how it feels to be unemployed and unable to buy your children Christmas presents. They know when not to shout. The president, the coolest man in the room, who worked among the unemployed in Chicago, knows too.

Joan Walsh's Twitter Brawl With Herself [1]

"I deeply resent people who insist that white progressives who criticize Obama are deluding themselves that they're his 'base,' when his 'base' is actually not white progressives, but people of color. Ishmael Reed laid out this pernicious line in December, in *The New York Times*, after many progressives, of every race, criticized Obama's tax cut compromise."

This was *Salon.com*'s Joan Walsh's response to my *Times* Op-Ed (12 December 2010) in which I expressed my dismay about a few media progressives referring to themselves as President Obama's base and voicing opposition to the president's policies without mentioning that Obama had majority support among blacks and Hispanics, but nowhere in the Op-Ed did I say that "people of color" were Obama's base.

Moreover, the Republican Party was threatening to halt the extension of unemployment benefits to thousands of workers unless the president went along with the tax cuts for their big business employers. Their Christmas gift to thousands of workers.

That took me back to a Christmas in 1966. I'd just received an advance for my first novel and sent some cash to my parents.

---

1. A version of this essay appeared at Counterpunch.org, May 3, 2011.

Unbeknownst to me, my stepfather's union was on strike and he'd been laid off. They didn't have the cash to buy my brothers and sister gifts and so the cash that I sent helped. My mother said that after the money arrived, she found my stepfather on the steps. He was weeping. I'd never known him to weep.

Wealthy white progressive women like those who interrupted the president's speech over the harsh conditions accorded Bradley Manning have the bread to buy Christmas gifts. (Not a peep from these wealthy donors about the horrendous conditions that thousands of blacks and Hispanics live under in California where conditions are so bad that a book about California prisons is called *The Golden Gulag*. The prison hospitals are so horrid that the federal government took them over. Governors Jerry Brown and Arnold Schwarzenegger fought the takeover of prison hospitals that one writer described as a form of torture.)

Some of the 574 who responded to Ms. Walsh's article, "Wisconsin, Obama and the Democrats' Future," (*Salon*, 5 April 2011), chided Ms. Walsh for neglecting to provide a link to my *Times* Op-Ed so that readers could judge for themselves about whether I had called "people of color" Obama's base.

On Saturday, April 9, 2011 02:07 PM ET, a blogger named Oblomova wrote:

Hack Work

Joan, I'm curious as to why you failed to include a link to Ishmael Reed's *New York Times* piece even though that seems to be the source of much of your angst on "who's the base?"

Maybe, just maybe, it's because Reed never ONCE said what you claimed—that Obama's base is "actually not white progressives, but people of color."

What Reed ACTUALLY wrote: "When these progressives refer to themselves as Mr. Obama's base, all they see is themselves. They ignore polls showing steadfast support for the president among blacks and Latinos." That quite explicitly does NOT say that, "only African Americans are the base."

I've included the link to Reed's piece so anyone still reading this can read it for themselves and determine whether you gave Reed a fair reading, or whether you engaged in self-pitying demagogic hackery.

I believe Mr. Reed and the readers of *Salon* deserve an apology for your vicious (or should that be "pernicious?") and deliberate misreading of his words. Of course, that might get in the way of the "But I'M the Victim!" narrative you're spinning here.

On April 7, Caitlin Dickson at *Atlantic Wire* declared Ms. Walsh the winner of the "Twitter Brawl" which drew some harsh comments about Ms. Walsh from bloggers like *angryblacklady*, and *truthrose*. Caitlin Dickson's declaring Ms. Walsh the winner, without having read my Op-Ed, is called a hometown decision in boxing.

Ms. Walsh wrote that she found the *Atlantic Wire*'s support "lovely." On April 17, Howard Kurtz on *Reliable Sources* also showed Ms. Walsh some more love, tossing her a cream puff question about the brawl. The segment was billed as the beltway media's ignoring a left-wing revolt against the president. Rachel Maddow and Ms. Walsh represented the revolt. Kurtz's problems with the president are pronounced (he still claims that during the campaign the media supported Obama when three studies that I cite in my book, *Barack Obama and the Jim Crow Media* dispute this claim). He asked:

> You got into a Twitter fight about this, on this very subject, did you not?
>
> WALSH: I did. I got into a couple of Twitter fights.
>
> I mean one thing that I do want to say is that we really can't generalize about the base. The thing about the Democratic Party right now is that there are a lot of bases. There are a lot of pieces of the Obama puzzle, so that, for example, African Americans tend to be pleased with him.
>
> Now his standing with African Americans dropped from the 90s to 85, the lowest it's been. That's very interesting to me. But for the most part, African Americans are happier than the rest of the base.

She said that African Americans are happier than the rest of the base, but went on to say that 79 to 85 percent of liberals are happy, which sounds pretty happy to me.

But despite the love from *The Atlantic Wire* and Howard Kurtz, the bloggers were relentless, prompting Ms. Walsh into a final attempt to pacify the blogger uprising by announcing that she had a black friend, maybe two. In 1999, Ms. Walsh got involved in what could be termed a racial scuffle. She praised then Mayor Jerry Brown for ending a system of "racial spoils" in Oakland.

By the time Mayor Brown left office, his developer friends and contributors had helped themselves to the spoils by plundering the Oakland treasury for the purpose of constructing ill-advised condo districts to accommodate Brown's "elegant density" without anticipating a burst in the housing market. He wanted ten thousand elegant (whites) to populate Oakland. Only five thousand have showed up. Half elegant?

As Gov. he gave a sweetheart deal to the powerful prison guards' union. They contributed two million to his campaign. Ms. Walsh also agreed with a black writer that the police who shot Amadou Diallo forty-one times were not murderers.

She finally apologized about her role in the twitter brawl, kinda. She said, "to the extent that I was at times unkind in this melee, I regret it." Not once, however, did she provide a link to my Op-Ed, which was the source of the blogger and twitter storm.

I actually like Joan Walsh. She invited me to lunch once. I think that she wanted me to write for *Salon*, but nothing came of it. I found her to be a pleasant and bright person, but I don't think that she anticipated the brawl that she sparked when she coupled "resent" with "people of color." (Maybe Ms. Walsh and her *Salon.com* colleague Laura Miller should invite me to lunch. They'd find that I'm really a nice person. Ms. Miller called my Mark Twain essay "rowdy" because I criticized her sisterhood buddy, Michiko Kakutani, a critic who has such a low opinion of blacks that she praised a stereotypes hall-of-fame contender written by a white girl, who claimed to have connections with black gangs and a character named "Big Mama." The memoir writer lied; the ghetto memoir was fake.)

Finally, the controversy raises two questions. Are wealthy advertising-rich dot.com sites bonding with corporate cable in an effort to stifle what they consider an impudent uprising from bloggers whose only assets are a laptop and Wi-Fi?

And after taking abuse from a Jim Crow media for a couple of hundred years, has cyberspace provided a blogger underclass with the ability to talk back? To be heard and not just seen? To have a voice instead of being confined to providing musical interludes between serious "progressive" talk, like in the movies where the folks were brought up to the big house to belt out a few numbers. Are we arriving at a time when we get the opinions of the rest of us without being interpreted and explained by intermediaries?

Brown Shirts, Black Shirts, T-Shirts[1]

On October 2, 2010, Litquake, a San Francisco literary movement founded by Jane Ganahl and Jack Boulware, held a tribute to poet Lawrence Ferlinghetti. Thousands showed up at the Herbst Theater to honor the ninety-year-old writer. Among those participating in the tribute were Juan Felipe Herrera, Jack Hirschman, devorah major, Patti Smith, Michael McClure, Winona Ryder and Robert Scheer. For my part, I saluted Lawrence Ferlinghetti as an American writer who saw through the glorification of an imperial president, whose words of peace are now used in commercial advertising. Even progressives and liberals have joined in on the celebration of a president whose warnings about a "military industrial complex" are quoted fondly even though he used the military to support the interests of industrialists like United Fruit. The actual phrase, 'military industrial complex,' was created by Emmett John Hughes, a speechwriter, but this appears to be all that a younger generation of historians and pundits remember about Dwight Eisenhower.

Steve Hayward, a fellow of the Claremont Institute, notes that "center-left thinkers" have begun to embrace former President Eisenhower, retrospectively, following the lead of Murray Kempton, the former writer for the pre-Murdoch liberal *New York Post*.

---

1. A version of this essay appeared at Counterpunch.org, November 2, 2011.

Around the same time, I tuned into the *Thom Hartmann Show* and heard Hartmann heap praise upon the former president. He was joined in this tribute by Peter Beinart, a writer for *The New Republic* magazine. Thom Hartmann is described as a progressive voice on radio and Beinart, a hawk, plays a liberal on the talk shows. Douglas Brinkley, a liberal historian, has compared Dwight Eisenhower to George Washington.

This is the Eisenhower who said that Asians had no regard for human life and who was constantly threatening Asian countries with "nuclear blackmail." He even suggested a target for a nuclear attack during the Korean War. The North Korean city of Kaesong.

Eisenhower wanted the Supreme Court to uphold *Plessy v. Ferguson*, the Jim Crow doctrine of separate but equal, and when Earl Warren went against his advice, Warren was never again invited to a White House reception.

This was the president who told nigger jokes to his golf partners. The Eisenhower who okayed the overthrow of an Iranian government replacing the elected leader, Dr. Mohammad Mossadegh, with the Shah, Mohammad Reza Shah Pahlavi Shahanshah, an act that has cost a resentment that we are still paying for in blood and treasure.

A covert operation under Eisenhower took out Jacobo Arbenz Guzmán, the elected head of Guatemala's government; he ordered that Air Force cover be provided for Arbenz's foes which led to the resignation of Arbenz. Eisenhower even tried to unseat the government of Indonesia. It was under the Eisenhower administration that the assassination of Patrice Lumumba and the invasion of Cuba were planned.

This was the president who wrote a glowing letter on behalf of the apartheid government of South Africa.

In 1958, President Eisenhower was viewed by most Americans as a Caesar, a god, and a man whom Douglas MacArthur said could become as admired as Jesus Christ if he ordered a nuclear field placed at the Yalu River, on the border between North Korea and China.

In 1958, Lawrence Ferlinghetti published *Tentative Description Of A Dinner Given to Promote The Impeachment of President Eisenhower*, a courageous act in the 1950s when those who opposed the government were considered Communists, the demonized entity of the day.

Therefore I was surprised when Lee Siegel, writing in *The New York Times Book Review*, made a bizarre attempt to link the Beats to the T-Shirts. He wrote "The Beats, though pacifist, were essentially apolitical."

Apolitical? He hasn't read Ted Joans, Bob Kaufman, Amiri Baraka, Allen Ginsberg and Ferlinghetti. Ginsberg's *Wichita Vortex Sutra*, which condemns war politicians by name, is one of the best antiwar poems. I asked Kerouac biographer Gerry Nicosia his opinion of the Siegel claim.

It is absurd to say the Beats were apolitical. The Beats—speaking now of Kerouac, Ginsberg, Burroughs, John Clellon Holmes, among others—were deeply shaped by World War II. They understood the necessity of fighting evil—Kerouac volunteered for the merchant marine—but they also believed that militarism for its own sake was a highly dangerous path and likely to become addictive to those in power. The Beats were, to a man and woman, appalled by the use of the atomic bomb against the Japanese, and they felt that the rapidly escalating buildup of American military armaments after World War II and the concomitant Cold War—with its threat of mutual destruction—was absolutely insane. Kerouac comments on the show of empty-headed military might in *On The Road* as Kerouac and Cassady drive through Washington, D.C. at the time of Truman's inauguration and Dean Moriarty (Neal Cassady) wonders why a good "man from Missouri" like Truman had "fallen asleep at the wheel." When Kerouac defined Beat Generation for John Clellon Holmes, he also talked about the need to transform America into a kinder and gentler nation (long before George H.W. Bush used it as a political catch phrase)—a nation that would welcome and try to understand other cultures and religions, not bomb them. Ginsberg's poem "Hum Bomb!" is of course the most obvious satire and condemnation of America's propensity to bomb rather than love and understand peoples who are different from us, but Ginsberg's whole career twined with antiwar activism—culminating with his great poem against the madness of the Vietnam War, "Wichita

Vortex Sutra." As for Burroughs, almost his entire oeuvre is about the misuse and abuse of power, the continual institution of control systems which limit human growth and fulfillment, and an exploration of the destructive effects of government on the course of human cultural evolution. If *Naked Lunch* were not so threatening to the established system of government, and to the constrainment of natural human behavior that government seeks to enforce, the U.S. government's strenuous efforts to suppress it would be almost incomprehensible.

Moreover, while the T-Shirts seek to cut off knowledge from the world by banning Ethnic Studies in Arizona, and banning the teaching of Islam in Texas (in the name of Western civilization about which they also lack knowledge), Allen Ginsberg, a Buddhist, and his followers were always known for their cosmopolitanism. A few years before his death, Ginsberg taught Black Literature at Brooklyn College; I was one of his guest lecturers.

All one has to do is read the ads for writing workshops, conferences, retreats, etc. carried in *Poets and Writers, The American Poetry Review,* and *AWP* to see that Naropa University, founded by Ginsberg and now run by poet Anne Waldman, is one of a handful that appreciates diversity beyond tokenism. The American literary scene is as white separatist as the Tea Party.

While the man who occupied the White House at the time enthralled the majority of Americans, Lawrence Ferlinghetti's document ends with Eisenhower's resignation.

Before I went onstage to offer my tribute, I ran into Robert Scheer backstage. He approached me to discuss my *CounterPunch* reference to remarks he'd made about mortgage foreclosures. He'd said on radio station KPFA that the banks extending loans to "the poor and drug addicts," which to me are code words, caused the economic collapse. In my article I cited studies from Brandeis and the Center for Responsible Lending, which accused the banks of engaging in racist practices by holding blacks and Hispanics to higher interest rates than whites. Scheer told me to read his book: *The Great American Stickup.*

I didn't think much of it until I heard Scheer on Berkeley's KPFA, FM, (10/09/10). He was answering some soft questioning by Aimee

Alison. While blasting Obama, Maxine Waters, and Jesse Jackson, Scheer had kind words for the Tea Party, America's equivalent of Hitler's Brown Shirts, and Mussolini's Black Shirts: the T-Shirts. He praised Rand Paul, a Medicare pimp, for his integrity. He's not the only progressive, or liberal who is getting all touchy feely about the T-Shirts.

Air America progressive Thom Hartmann is on board. Also the kind of person who is described as a "responsible conservative" in the neo-Nazi handbook, *The Turner Diaries*, Ross Gregory Douthat, a Pentecostal turned Catholic, who is present on the *Times*' editorial page to present red meat (choice cuts, not like the maggot infested brand over at Fox) to Red State subscribers. He says that those who accuse the T-Shirts of racism have it wrong. "The 'tea partiers are racists' theory is the most inflammatory story line, but there are many more."

Inflammatory? Not according to a 92-page report prepared by Devin Burghart and Leonard Zeskind from the Institute for Research & Education on Human Rights, serious scholars, who, unlike some pundits, don't just make remarks originating in their lower digestive tracts. Some of their findings:

> Tea Party leaders have promoted and provided a platform to known racists and anti-Semites on multiple occasions. Dale Robertson, the chairman of the 1776 who displayed the infamous "n****r sign," for example, brought Martin 'Red' Beckman on as a guest to the *Tea Party Radio* hour that he co-hosts with Washington state talk show host Dr. Laurie Roth. Beckman has been known for over twenty-five years for his anti-Semitic writings and his defense of militias. In 1994, Beckman was evicted from his property in Montana by the IRS for refusing to pay taxes. He now resides in southwestern Washington state.

> [John] Weaver, of Fitzgerald, Georgia, has a sprawling set of connections to neo-Confederates and those preaching the so-called Christian Identity doctrine. He is the former chaplain in chief of the Sons of Confederate Veterans. He has spoken at "Christian Identity" gatherings in Branson, Missouri, in 1998 and 1999. According to this particular theology, Jews are considered a satanic force (or the incarnation of Satan himself), and people of color are considered less than fully human.

The list of out-front anti-Semites on Tea Party platforms includes an event in July 2009. One thousand people gathered in Upper Senate Park for a rally in D.C. A full line-up of speakers included representatives from several tax reform groups, FreedomWorks, and talk show hosts. Also on the platform that day was the band Poker Face, playing music, providing technical back up, and receiving nothing but plaudits from the crowd. The band, from Lehigh Valley, Pennsylvania, already had a reputation for anti-Semitism. Lead singer Paul Topete was on the public record calling the Holocaust a hoax, and writing and performing for *American Free Press*—a periodical published by Willis Carto, the godfather of Holocaust denial in the United States.

One of the most zealous white nationalists visible in Tea Party circles has been Billy Joe Roper, Jr. A former Russellville, Arkansas high school teacher, Roper was an enrolled member of the ResistNet Tea Party. He is also running a write-in campaign for Arkansas governor. Roper's views are unabashed. A one-time leader of the National Alliance, an organization dedicated to the creation of an all-white country and the requisite expulsion and/or murder of Jews and people of color, he continues to idolize its founder, William Pierce. Pierce authored *The Turner Diaries*, a race-war terror novel carried around by Oklahoma City bomber Timothy McVeigh.

And so with people with such backgrounds playing a prominent role in the Tea Party, where does Matt Bai in the Sunday *Times* (October 31, 2010) get off comparing the T-Shirts with MoveOn? Has anybody from MoveOn ever stomped somebody in the head? Or threatened to set up a white separate nation by force?

Or Lee Siegel comparing the T-Shirts with the Beats? Did Allen Ginsberg ever handcuff a journalist? What is it with this cowardly media, so scared that they're going to be swiftboated like Dan Rather, posing such bizarre equivalencies like Stewart/Colbert comparing Keith Olbermann and Ed Shultz with Glenn Beck and Bill O'Reilly, whose ravings have inspired people to murder three Pittsburgh policemen and a doctor who provided women with abortions. After the Civil War, Frederick Douglass complained about a consensus that said both sides, the South and the North, fought for just causes.

Apparently Sam Hitchmough writing in *CounterPunch* and Lee Siegel, of *The New York Observer*, writing in *The New York Times Book Review*, weren't aware of what was crawling beneath the T-Shirt rock. And why are Siegel and David Brooks so comfortable with the T-Shirts among whose prominent members are Holocaust deniers? Does this come under the heading of the *Fatal Embrace*, from the brilliant book by the same name by Benjamin Ginsburg?

Finally, at *Counterpunch*, Patrick Brennan defended the T-Shirts against Matt Taibbi's article in *The Rolling Stone*, but I think that I'll go with Taibbi, Burghart and Zeskind's view of the T-Shirts. They say that they're against socialism but none of the spokespersons for the Tea Party factions who withered before Lawrence O'Donnell's unsparing questioning on his MSNBC show on October 28, 2010, seem to know what it meant. Representatives of Tea Party Nation, Freedom Works, FedUpUSA and the Tea Party Express answered no when asked by Lawrence O'Donnell whether they would end Social Security and Medicare. Ending Medicare would prevent some of the T-Shirts from getting to rallies using scooters paid for by the government.

Yet, Judson Phillips of Tea Party Nation said that a hatred for socialism was what glued the different party factions. No it's not socialism, but the president's black face that has gotten them energized and some progressives refuse to see that because they're high on the post-race opiate. They see class, gender or sexual orientation as the "restrictive factors" in American life.

No, T-Shirts are not against big government and calling them the silent majority is a stretch and another example of the media's boosting the T-Shirts beyond their influence because people acting crazy is good copy. And when faced with some tough questioning by O'Donnell, their pretenses collapsed.

So I'm not taking the word on T-Shirts from the opinion of liberals and progressives and responsible conservatives.

I'm suggesting that blacks and Hispanics wear hardhats when they go vote so that when the T-Shirts' "voter-integrity squads" invade our neighborhoods to monitor us, we won't suffer brain damage when they stomp us on our heads.

Ethnic Studies in the Age
of the Tea Party[1]

In the 1980s, I met with Czech writers who used the word *Samisdat* to describe an underground movement of poets who defied the censorship polices of the Soviet occupation. This reminded me of Richard Wright's stealthy attempts to acquire literacy in the segregated South, the black part of which was under occupation by white supremacists, who controlled the political and cultural life of blacks as a result of terrorism, the history of which has been ignored by American schoolbooks.[2] There has been a history of censorship of literary expression by blacks and by those who were sympathetic to the emancipation of blacks—Andrew Jackson ordered the censorship of abolitionist pamphlets.[3]

My School Curricula

Black literature, though available in the 1940s and 1950s, when I attended school, was absent from the school curriculum. I was one of

---

1. A version of this article appeared in *American Studies/Amerikastudienin,* Universitatsverlag Heidelberg, Volume 55, Number 4, 2010.
2. Richard Wright, *Black Boy,* chapter 13, in Rampersad 233-37. Wright had to forge notes to the library in order not to be detected as the book borrower.
3. "Jackson's administration directed postmasters not to deliver the controversial tracts and encouraged Congress to outlaw 'incendiary' anti-slavery literature as a public safety measure." *Andrew Jackson, A Life,* A PBS Special produced by Redhill Productions and Community Television of Southern California.

those young persons who was lucky enough to have access to Mary Crosby Chappelle, a historic civil rights leader, who served the Buffalo community until she died at the age of one hundred, and A.J. Smitherman, who produced a newspaper called *The Empire Star* in Buffalo, New York, where Ms. Chappelle worked. He also wrote poetry. I didn't know it at the time, but learned years later that he was the primary target of mob violence and accused of sparking the worst riot in American history, the Tulsa Oklahoma Riot of 1921. It began when Smitherman, publisher of *The Tulsa Star*, and other armed black men offered help to a sheriff who was holding off a mob that was threatening to lynch a black boy who was accused of raping a white girl (regardless of the speculation that they were lovers).[4] It was these writers and Smitherman's son Toussaint, a linotypist, who introduced me to black history.

Although the work of Richard Wright was not available to me, black newspapers like *The Afro-American*, *The Chicago Defender* and *The Pittsburgh Courier* were. And I didn't have to sneak and read them by flashlight even though they offered views some considered objectionable. Unlike today's black points of view, which might be managed by multi-millionaires like Arianna Huffington, or think tanks like the Manhattan Institute, or right-wing editors, who might accost them in private with racist jibes, the black press was so independent that J. Edgar Hoover wanted to charge them with sedition.[5]

---

4. See Ellsworth, *Death in a Promised Land: The Tulsa Race Riot of 1921* (Scholarly, 2002). In keeping with the tradition practiced by some white newspapers of advocating the lynching, or even the extermination of blacks and Indians, *The Tulsa Tribune* started rumors of a lynching of the accused rapist, "Diamond" Dick Rowland. *The Tribune* carried the headline, "To Lynch Negro Tonight." A.J. Smitherman declared, "There is no crime, however atrocious, that justifies mob violence" (44). Ellsworth's book reports that, "there is no real evidence that Dick Rowland attempted to assault Sarah Page" (46). After the massacre, Smitherman and his family had to flee from Oklahoma. The state of Massachusetts refused to extradite him to Oklahoma where he was charged with sedition. Sarah Page refused to prosecute. Dick Rowland was posthumously exonerated in 2008.
5. See Washburn, Patrick S., *A Question of Sedition: The Federal Government's Investigation of the Black Press During World War II.* New York: Oxford

I worked in the office of *The Empire Star* in high school and, after dropping out of college, returned to write for the newspaper. As a result, I met Malcolm X, who told me that black history as it was taught was "cotton patch history." This was his answer to me after I'd asked him whether his opinion of black history was that it had been "distorted." Malcolm X and the Southern students who came to Buffalo to work during the summer knew more about black history than we, suggesting that Black Studies began at historically black colleges in the South. One of those students was William H. Peace, co-editor of *The Angry Black South: Southern Negroes Tell Their Own Story* (1962)—one of the first books to alert the nation to the rising protests on the part of students at black Southern colleges. Another product of a black college was Charles Harris, who became an editor at Random House. He startled a room full of white editors when he mentioned that blacks fought in the Civil War. They had been indoctrinated by the same curricula as we: curricula based upon the notion that only the history and culture of 'white' people were worthy of study and among these only certain 'white' people.

Before I began working for *The Empire Star*, I remember buying a copy of Joel A. Rogers's *100 Amazing Facts about the Negro with Complete Proof: A Shortcut to the World History of the Negro* (1957) in a second-hand bookstore. This pamphlet was my first introduction to African-American history. I took it to school and mentioned some of the facts in a classroom. The teacher dismissed the pamphlet with a wave of a hand. The situation didn't change at the University of Buffalo, which was an expensive private university before it became SUNY Buffalo. Except for a class in linguistics taught by Henry Lee Smith, Ray L. Birdwhistell, and George L. Trager, there wasn't a single reference to black history or culture. Dr. Trager

University Press, 1986. More recently, Carole Simpson, former NBC and ABC correspondent, had to self-publish her memoir, *NewsLady* (2010), because it exposes the racism, humiliation, sexual harassment, sexual aggression, and stereotyping that black women must endure while working in the news media. She also details how she was betrayed by a white woman and a black man who were promoted through her efforts.

offered to discuss a linguistic map of Africa, but none of the students was interested, including me. I figured that assimilation was my ticket out of my working-class background and into the middle class.

I remember a very popular history professor named Selig Adler,[6] who, in a lecture, dismissed the underground railroad as "a myth," when Buffalo played a key role in the anti-slavery movement and visible remains of the underground railroad existed in a church that was located on Michigan Avenue. The home of its pastor, Rev. J. Edward Nash, is now a museum. Rev. Nash's church was a historic landmark because fugitive slaves used to hide there en route to Canada. Not until I began to research the history of Buffalo for my novel *Flight to Canada* (1976) did I become aware of Buffalo's role in black history, one of the last stops before Canada. William Wells Brown, an early black writer, lived there. I'm still learning. Only recently did I discover that nineteenth-century novelist and soldier, advocate of emigration and Lincoln guest, Martin Robison Delany, attended a convention of the Free Soil Party in Buffalo, where Martin Van Buren was chosen as the party's candidate for president. None of this was available in Buffalo's school curriculum, neither at the grammar and high school, nor the university level. Instead, Paris and London were the cities that we were encouraged to study.

In the view of these educators, history and culture began with the Greeks and, before that, people went shambling and grunting about. Of course the Greeks were more cosmopolitan than the educators, who still view themselves as part of an overseas colony of settlers. Not only was the history of blacks excluded but also that of white ethnics. It was only through Jewish, Irish, and Italian intellectuals, who were members of the Before Columbus Foundation, that I did become acquainted with other lost histories and cultures.

When I began to connect with writers of other ethnic backgrounds in the late 1960s, I found that my experience wasn't unique.

---

6. Selig Adler (1909-1984) authored books about American isolationism and foreign policy as well as *From Ararat ta Suburbia: The History of the Jewish Community in Buffalo* (1960).

Novelist Shawn Wong said that during his four years at the University of California at Berkeley not once was a text by a Chinese-American author used in a classroom. I spent part of a summer living in the Alaska home of Alfred Perkins, traditional chief of the Tlingit Frog Clan. He said that when members of his community attended school, they were punished for speaking in their language. The goal of the education of African Americans, Asian Americans, Native Americans, and Hispanics was to assimilate them into a culture where all of the great storytelling was done by white men. They had to learn what Matthew Arnold called "the best that has been thought and said in the world" (*Culture and Anarchy* [1869]) and submit to an education that promised that intelligence could be had by gaining a superficial knowledge of the traditions of a handful of Western countries. (When I taught at the University of California at Berkeley, I tested the students' knowledge of "Western Civilization" by asking them to write about a European myth, non-Roman and non-Greek. Through this assignment, they discovered that they were only acquainted with a fraction of Europe's history and culture.)

I figured that having devoted the first eighteen years of my life to studying European literature, art, and music, even performing in a string quartet dedicated to playing classical European music, I was ready for something different. I was about nineteen when I stumbled upon works of James Baldwin while working at a library. Reading this black author inspired me to think that perhaps I could become a writer. I went to New York at the age of twenty-two. Again, I was lucky. A new Renaissance was stirring. Writers, artists, and musicians were gathering in the East Village. I joined the Umbra workshop and was introduced to works that had been absent from the schools and lectures to which I had been exposed from early grades to the university. But as the co-founder of *The East Village Other*, an early underground newspaper, which I named, I also had a foot in the white counterculture and was cited as one of three of its favorite writers in the official Woodstock program. It was in New York that I was introduced to black nationalism. I say introduced because nobody told me that the church in which I became a youth leader,

the A.M.E. Zion Church, was a black-nationalist church that was
formed as a result of the racist practices of the white Methodist
church. The A.M.E. Zion Church buried Harriet Tubman.[7]

Black New York intellectuals were building a reading list that
would be part of a Black Enlightenment that was spreading across
the country. This list, captured in Eugene Redmond's *Drumvoices*
(1976), included works by both black and white authors. One of the
handbooks of the New York black-nationalist movement was *Muntu*
(1961), written by Janheinz Jahn, a tall, blue-eyed, blonde German
whom I accompanied on his rounds in New York one day.

Umbra poets were published in *Liberator* and *New Masses* magazines. There were poetry readings up- and downtown. I met Langston
Hughes, Ralph Ellison, James Baldwin. Hughes was responsible for
my first novel getting published. Amiri Baraka read my poetry and
made comments about it. "You have your own thing," he said. Except
for Tom Dent and Calvin Hernton, now icons, most of those who
were members of the workshop had been compelled to submit to a
curriculum that viewed Europe as the center of the intellectual
universe.

The Beginnings of Black Studies

White supremacists were devoted to something they called "Western
Civilization," which, without the intervention of Muslim scholars,
would not exist.[8] They were faced with a revolt in the 1960s, which

---

7. "However, the A.M.E. Zion Church became known as the freedom church
because it was the spiritual home for some of the most famous of the freedom
movement, Frederick Douglass, Harriet Tubman and Sojourner Truth" (*The
African Church in the African American Experience*, C. Eric Lincoln and
Lawrence H. Mamiya, p. 202).

8. "In 1231 Pope Gregory IX convened a special commission to decide which
parts of Aristotle were worth preserving and which weren't [...] But try as the
church might, the study of Aristotle went on clandestinely. So did the study of
his commentator Ibn Rushd [Averroes], the one who translated him, explained
him and made him live." (Graham 113).

they resisted at first but then complied with through some modest reforms. Dr. Nathan Hare is correct in his assertion that Black Studies were begun in historically black colleges in the South.[9] Through the agitation of black scholars like Nathan Hare at San Francisco State and the Black Panthers at Merritt College, located across the street from the house where Bobby Seale, co-founder of the Black Panthers, still lives, courses in black literature were established in the West as well. I asked Bobby Seale and Nathan Hare what it was like when the demand for Black Studies sometimes led to violence.

Just as a few low-budget experiments by musicians like Ike Turner led to the founding of the multi-billion-dollar rock and roll industry, a thirty-five-dollar library card became seed money for the foundation of one of the first modern Black Studies programs at Merritt College in Oakland, California. The card belonged to Bobby Seale, an engineer who worked on the Gemini project and later founded the Black Panther Party. Like rock and roll, Black Studies would create a payroll of millions of dollars for colleges and universities and a bonanza of book sales for the publishing industry.

One could say that the Western phase of the Black Enlightenment Movement began off campus, just like the French Enlightenment (Voltaire, for example, was a playwright). Seale's using a U.C. Berkeley library card, even though he was not enrolled there, enabled him to assemble materials that would form the basis for a Black Studies course. He says that the 26 libraries of U.C. Berkeley became his "research stomping ground" and the discussions about how to design the initial courses took place, not on campus, but in Bobby Seale's Oakland home.[10] The meetings were attended by over a dozen people called the Black History Fact Group, who were assigned by Seale to create a synopsis about aspects of African-American history. They came up with a syllabus that involved four courses, two in African Studies and two in African-American Studies. Melville

---

9. Author exchanged e-mail with Hare on January 21, 2011.
10. Seale in phone conversation with the author, February 2011.

Herskovits, W.E.B. Du Bois, Carter Godwin Woodson, Herbert Aptheker, Lorenzo Dow Turner, and Lerone Bennett, Jr., were among those authors whose books Seale borrowed from U.C. Berkeley's libraries. They were supplemented by suggestions made by members of the Black History Fact Group. Armed with their syllabi, Seale and his group confronted the Merritt College administration, which was represented by Dean Olson. At first, he dismissed the Black History Fact Group as "a bunch of unnecessary black militants."[11] But when Seale showed up with 200 students and threatened to shut down the campus, Olson and the administration changed their minds. The first course in African-American Studies at Merritt began in the fall of 1965 and was taught by Rodney P. Carlisle, a white instructor. The creation of Black Studies at Merritt, Seale told me, was inspired by the death on February 21, 1965, of Malcolm X, whose critical comment about Black history being "cotton patch history" was certainly borne out by how it was represented in our schoolbooks: contented slaves dancing barefoot to the fiddle.

Nathan Hare sent me a response to my inquiry on January 21, 2011:

> As for whether black studies came first at Merritt or San Francisco State, it depends on what you mean by 'black studies.' If you mean some courses with black or African content or focus you might say Merritt, but the HBCUs [historically black colleges and universities] had courses in the South for decades before Merritt College was born. I recollect that Merritt College never had a department of black studies but a Center for Ethnic Studies starting about 1972. This is all off the top of my head. I don't believe that Merritt College has a black studies program now; they have what they call 'African-American' studies (presumably aiming to be more white-friendly).

> 'Black studies' got its impetus as a movement and an entity at San Francisco State. Some of the students of necessity had gone to Merritt, which probably led to the myth of the Merritt origin. Jimmy Garrett, who took the educational efforts of such as Maryanna Waddy, the La Brie brothers, and members of the Black Arts Movement, got with

---

11. Seale in phone conversation with the author, Feb. 2011.

George Murray, not Huey Newton, of the Black Panthers, and forged
the 'black studies movement.' They did not attend Merritt, as I recollect
it, but the community college in Los Angeles before coming to San
Francisco State, and the rest is history. San Francisco State was where
black studies became a movement that electrified the nation. I believe
Maulana Karenga, who had a formidable place himself in the origins
of the black studies movement, has continued to maintain, in all editions of his seminal textbook,[12] that black studies as such originated at
San Francisco State. Why is it when we were getting the black studies
program going at San Francisco State we never thought of calling on
Merritt College for input or for a model though we were friendly with
their faculty and some of them were advocates of black studies and by
then taught courses? Indeed I recall speaking at a meeting of a confer-
ence at Merritt College when a Merritt College official stood arguing
against the idea of a black studies course that only blacks could attend
(something that was an issue on San Francisco State's campus the day
I arrived) though its president was sponsoring and monitoring the
meeting. I remember telling a student from Yale or somewhere who
was arguing for a black university that right now we're trying to get
courses started. Some of the black orientation then seems unnecessar-
ily separatist now but it seemed necessary then to break away from
integrationism and assimilationism. Mao also thought the revolution
was a two-step process, with nationalism being the first stage. Bear in
mind, as quiet as it is kept, that the rallies for separatist black studies
at San Francisco State each day during the five-month strike consisted
predominantly of white people, although the speakers were all black.
Note that when five hundred and fifty-seven people were arrested one
day at San Francisco State, most of the people arrested were white.
Indeed in my large holding cell of about thirty people, only one other
person was black. Speaking of the idea of a black university, we thought
we were inventing something when we fought to make Howard a black
university in 1966 and 1967. Later I learned that a white man, the first
president of Howard [Charles B. Boynton, who took office on March
19, 1867] was forced to resign because he wanted Howard to focus on
blackness and the glories of ancient Africa and the like, while General

---

12. Maulana Karenga, *Introduction to Black Studies* (Los Angeles: University of
Sankore Press 1982). The book is now in its fourth edition

Howard, president of the board of trustees and his replacement as president, wanted an integrationist institution.

This is why I don't like to get into origins of black education because you're liable to run into a white man. For instance, Melville Herskovits started an 'Afroamerican Studies' program in 1947; African studies in 1957. I participated in an argument that ran through most of the day one Saturday at San Francisco State in 1968 over whether to change and call black studies 'Afroamerican studies' (as some institutions call it now). I argued to keep 'black studies.' Maryanna Waddy, who lays some claim and will tell you she started black studies, was a leader of the Afroamerican studies faction. By the way, 'ethnic studies' did not start at Merritt either. When I first came to San Francisco State Jimmy Garrett took me to a meeting of the [all white] Academic Senate. There they were speaking of starting 'minority studies' programs. I remarked that I didn't like the word 'minority,' that black people are more oppressed where and when we're in the majority (Rhodesia as against Sweden, Mississippi as against Maine) than when we're in the minority. The dean said, 'what should we call it?' I said, 'For want of a better word, 'ethnic studies'. Hope this helps. (e-mail to the author; see Hare and Hare; Seale).

The revolt that was begun at San Francisco State and Merritt spread to other colleges and universities in the West. In the summer of 1967, I left New York for Los Angeles, where I, without an automobile, was holed up in an apartment; there I wrote the major part of my second novel, *Yellow Back Radio Broke-Down* (1969). That fall, I traveled to San Francisco to promote my first novel, *The Free-Lance Pallbearers* (1967). Hearing that I was living in Berkeley, Thomas Parkinson, a professor in Berkeley's English Department, invited me to teach a course in African-American literature. He'd reviewed the novel on KPFA radio. I taught the first course in African-American literature at Berkeley. (One of the texts I used was *Invisible Man* to determine what critics meant when they said that my first novel was influenced by Ellison's book.) On the first day of the class, I got a sampling of the resistance met by Nathan Hare and others when they sought to get Black Studies adopted by San Francisco State. Two white women came in to ask why a course in African-

American literature was necessary when we already had James Baldwin. I'd heard the same thing in the East Village from members of the counterculture: that they already had a black writer.

Later, many white women would be influenced by Alicia Ostriker's *Stealing the Language: The Emergence of Women's Poetry in America* (1986). Just as the modern feminist movement would be influenced by SNCC (Student Nonviolent Coordinating Committee), Black Studies led to the creation of Ethnic Studies and Women's Studies, Queer Studies and all of the other Studies that had been excluded from the curriculum before then. Affirmative Action, stereotyped by the media and even by Professor John McWhorter as a black program, increased the presence of white women on U.C. Berkeley's campus. Professor Charles Henry of the African American Studies Department wrote about the consequences for women faculty of Proposition 209, which banned Affirmative Action. His article "Gender Equity Issues at U.C. Berkeley" states:

> What is the status of women faculty members on this campus? On the positive side, the numbers have grown from 11% of the ladder-rank faculty in 1981 to 18% in 1991 and almost 25% in 2000. The availability pool of women with doctorates has also increased during this period and now represents over 30% of all Ph.D.'s nationally. In fact, this past year approximately 40% of all doctorates went to women. There were also gains in professional staff representation. Today, about 63% of UC-Berkeley's professional staff are women. Unfortunately, continued growth in these positive numbers is threatened and may even be reversed. The hiring rate for women who are new hires has dropped from 33% of the total hires before Proposition 209 to 27% after Proposition 209.

In his book *Dude, Where's My Black Studies Department* (2007), Cecil Brown claims that overseas blacks, who were considered less confrontational than black Americans, were brought in to man and woman these departments, an attempt, as he sees it, to tamp down the revolt. He claims that Diaspora Studies has been designed to weaken the influence of African-American intellectuals and scholars. But both African and African-American scholars don't have the power or the influence to chart the course of the American curriculum as do the people who run the universities and colleges.

The Age of the Tea Party

The hysteria that has accompanied the election of a black president has led to the rise of a well-funded mob called the Tea Party, which seems to include every Holocaust denier and neo-Nazi who has been on the hate circuit for the last few decades.[13] For them the president is a "Witch Doctor," "Alien," "Muslim," and someone whose birth certificate is counterfeit. While the more refined elements of academia have sought to moderate the revolt that began in the 1960s to challenge the curriculum and the canon, the Tea Party's challenge to Ethnic Studies has all of the subtlety of a dog fight.

Though progressives and others view the Tea Party as a grassroots uprising against Wall Street, the 2010 midterm elections revealed this to be a sham. They claim that their fear is based upon a country heading toward socialism, but most of them would not give up their entitlements. This anti-Washington movement sent lobbyists and senators who are close to lobbyists to Washington. In Florida, they elected a governor who took the Fifth Amendment over twenty times when charged with Medicare fraud, Rick Santelli, who refers to himself as the Tea Party's "lightning rod," made blatantly racist appeals during a rant offered on the floor of the Chicago mercantile exchange. (Ralph Waldo Emerson, an Anglo-Saxon supremacist, would probably be appalled by an Italian-American leader of a white supremacist faction.) This rant aimed at the black president implied that the president's policies would require whites to bail out blacks for taking out mortgages they couldn't afford, a myth refuted by economist Paul Krugman. Even *The Wall Street Journal* noted that over sixty percent of those who were lured into sub-prime loans were

---

13. See David Burghart and Leonard Zeskind's "Tea Party Nationalism," a report that names the Neo Nazis and Holocaust deniers who are playing a prominent role in the Tea Party.

eligible for conventional loans (as quoted in *Broke USA*, Gary Rivlin, p. 300).

It's not surprising that a movement obsessed with a black president, a black attorney general (the black police fantasy of the ultra right whose idea of a dystopia is one in which Jews take away the guns of white men, making their homes defenseless against invasions from black savages) and a movement in which Holocaust deniers and neo-Nazis play a prominent role would present Ethnic Studies with its most serious challenge. The Tea Party and the monopoly media that spawned it have aroused such fear in millions of white Americans that they have retreated to the cultural and political covered wagons where they feel besieged by the Others who, in their minds, are war-whooping and showering them with arrows of political correctness. The fear is whipped up by media pundits and public intellectuals who are backed by billions of dollars from corporations. Ethnic Studies has been outlawed in Arizona and is under attack in Texas, where school boards are recommending that Thomas Jefferson be demoted and Jefferson Davis be elevated (and maybe John Wilkes Booth?). The Tennessee Tea Party is proposing that the issue of slavery be eliminated from textbooks.

You would think that the white liberal intelligentsia would launch a fierce counter attack on such ignorance. You would think they would check the attempt on the part of those who claim that the earth is six thousand years old to dictate the school curriculum. Given the power of the Texas school board to whose suggestions the textbook industry submits, aren't liberals and progressives alarmed by the prospect of their children being guided by textbooks influenced by people who believe that if you reached to a certain point in the world you would drop off into the abyss? Author Carla Blank learned of the power of Texas to influence the school curriculum in the early 1990s when her textbook was published:

> Dale Seymour Publications, an educational publisher now a Pearson Education imprint but then an independent press in Palo Alto, accepted the performing arts manuscript that I co-authored with Jody Roberts. The Dale Seymour editors explained that they wanted to enter our book

into the Texas adoption process, for consideration as a middle school textbook. If chosen, that would mean considerable income to the publisher and us, for at least the next five years, as Texas is the most populated state which mandates statewide textbook adoptions, and adoptions remain in place for a minimum of five years. Since our manuscript had been written as a teachers' guide for classrooms covering a much more comprehensive range, this resulted in considerable rewriting. We had carefully written the book to be consistent with standard professional theater practices besides the guidelines recommended by the National Endowment for the Arts, and now we had to also be sure we were consistent with the state of Texas' guidelines in our rush to meet their deadline. Strangely, our publisher decided to save money and not to do a hardcover edition of our text, now titled *Live On Stage!*, which made us ineligible for consideration under the Texas system. The book that won was not consistent with professional theater practices in our experiences, but it was published by a Texas company and displayed a huge Texas-style lone star on its cover.[14]

Why isn't there an outcry from the liberal establishment over the state of Texas's influence over what students read? The problem is that their grasp of American culture and history is about as weak as that of members of the Tea Party. Is there a Pulitzer Prize division of the Tea Party?

Reviewing a musical called *Bloody Bloody Andrew Jackson*, the influential public intellectual Jon Meacham, whose biography of Andrew Jackson, *American Lion*, was awarded the 2009 Pulitzer Prize, failed to mention Jackson's role as one of the most prominent slaveholders in the Southeast and as a president who encouraged the expansion of slavery into Texas. Meacham calls Jackson a "rock star."[15] The late historian Shelby Foote's white-washing of General Nathan Forrest is being invoked by white Mississippians who wish to make license plates honoring the general who has been accused

---

14. Carla Blank in conversation with the author, Feb. 2011.

15. Meacham writes: "Roughly put, the Jackson movement was to American politics in the 1820s and '30s what rock'n'roll was to American culture in the 1950s and '60s: young, raw, unsettling. Was Jackson a rock star? Yes [...]" ("Rocking the Vote").

of murdering black troops at Fort Pillow, even after their surrender. This deed has been called "the atrocity of the war" (Urwin 19). Pulitzer Prize winner Foote, whose grandfather was Jewish, compared the Ku Klux Klan, which engaged in massacres and the lynching of blacks, with the French Resistance (Adams). Foote also said that the KKK was prophetic in its prediction that blacks would behave as though they were "somewhere between ape and man" (Horwitz 153), which is ironic because this was the description of the Irish by their British critics.[16] All of the founders of the Klan were Scotch-Irish, who've been the subject of incest libel by others. Benjamin Franklin called them "white savages."

The phasing out of Ethnic Studies is a huge step backwards in American intellectual life. In Texas, the teaching of Arabic is forbidden, as is the study of Islam, cutting off the students' knowledge of a religion whose followers number a billion.[17] Of course, a recent survey revealed that most Americans don't have the rituals and history of Christianity quite nailed.[18] At its highest point, Ethnic Studies

---

16. "'The Klan takes some careful talking about, it's easy to misinterpret what I'm fixing to say', [Shelby] Foote cautioned." "'But in some ways the Klan was very akin to the Free French Resistance to Nazi occupation. To expect people who fought as valiantly as these people did to roll over and play dead because there was an occupying army is kind of crazy.'" "Foote also admired Nathan Bedford Forrest, the Klan's first Imperial Wizard, a slave trader before the War, and a rebel commander who allegedly permitted the slaughter of surrendering black troops at a battle called Fort Pillow" (see Horwitz, ch. "At the Foote of the Master," 153).

17. The Mansfield school district has backed off plans for an Arabic studies program after almost 200 parents showed up with questions at a meeting at Cross Timbers Intermediate School on Monday night (see Rogers).

18. "More than four-in-ten Catholics in the United States (45 %) do not know that their church teaches that the bread and wine used in Communion do not merely symbolize but actually become the body and blood of Christ. About half of Protestants (53 %) cannot correctly identify Martin Luther as the person whose writings and actions inspired the Protestant Reformation, which made their religion a separate branch of Christianity. Roughly four-in-ten Jews (43 %) do not recognize that Maimonides, one of the most venerated rabbis in history, was Jewish" (Pew Research Center).

led thousands of students out of their experience and backgrounds. They delved into the study of cultures, information that had been absent in the earlier grades.

I recall one memorable evening while I was a visiting lecturer at Washington & Lee University. I had just given a reading. On the stage behind me was a sarcophagus holding the remains of Robert E. Lee, whose reputation as a loser among Southerners was redeemed when a cult of his admirers made him president of this school.[19] During a reception, a white Citadel cadet approached me. He could have been Stonewall Jackson's twin, including the beard. He introduced himself. During the course of the conversation he began quoting passages from Jean Toomer's *Cane*. From memory.

19. See Connelly, *The Marble Man* (1978). The book argues that his contemporaries blamed Lee for losing the war. He was redeemed when he was installed as president of Washington & Lee University as a result of the fervor among a cult of his admirers. Another 'Lost Cause' fantasist is Winston Groom, whose novel *Forrest Gump*, adapted for the movies, was a modern reading of the 'Lost Cause,' and Reconstruction. In the movie, the U.S. defeat in Vietnam becomes the 'Lost Cause' and Reconstruction is represented by a white woman, who is corrupted by black men only to be rescued by Gump, whose first name Forrest seeks to present a comfy portrait of one of the most notorious of Confederate killers.

A Fly on the Wall[1]

(*Bar near the Capitol Building. Two southern Tea Party members. Sitting at the bar. A quarter bottle of Jim Beam in front of them. They have the style of the traveling salesmen made famous in the 1968 Maysles brothers' film,* Salesman. *Like other Tea Party congressmen, they're given to excessive smirks.*)

T-A: That fucking Boehner, McConnell and Cantor. Sold us out.

T-B: You telling me. We had a chance to keep a coon out of the White House for the next hundred years. Burn down the world economy like Sherman burned down Atlanta. Blame it on him.

T-A: Could have done the job that the coward Lee couldn't do in Gettysburg. You see how nervous these Yankees got about the prospect of a default.

T-B: I'll drink to that. (*They bump their glasses.*)

T-A: I'm beginning to think—no—.

T-B: No, say it, what's on your mind?

T-A: (*Whispers.*) That's not a tan. Boehner is a jungle bunny like Obama. These two are probably laughing at us while shooting dice in the family quarters. Can you imagine. The Kenyan and his Sambo family eatin' watermelon in space that was once occupied by…by… Ronald Reagan.

---

1. A version of this sketch appeared at Counterpunch, August 15, 2011.

(They pause. Become distant. Misty eyed.)

T-B: I can understand Cantor, the Yid, he's serving his international banking buddies, but what about McConnell? I thought he was on our side. He's a white man. A Southerner like us.

T-A: Look who he's married to. That's all you need to know.

T-B: Oh, right. Why didn't I think of that? A Chink.

T-A: She's probably got a chip stored in the frames of his bi-focals and passing all of the information on to the Reds. Hell, he might be a Manchurian candidate. That's why he was against the default, because China would lose a couple of trillion.

T-B: I never thought of it that way. The people in Louisiana were right to elect a genius like you.

T-A: And Tennessee, you.

(They bump glasses. Progressive Congressman Drew Foss approaches. Elegantly dressed. Cufflinks. Expensive cologne. Has had a few martinis. Puts his hand on T-A's shoulder, but seeing T-A gives his hand a hostile glance, removes it.)

Drew Foss: You fellas represent the working class's struggle against Wall Street. So do my people. Some call you racists but I defend you. These are paranoid people who are always playing the race card. We should join forces. Why, I just had a nice talk with Rand Paul. We see eye to eye on a lot of things. Why even Jane Hamsher and Grover Norquist are running buddies. Here's my card. Call me. (*Walks away.*)

T-A: (*Mocks him.*) Here's my card. Call me. Must be some kind of fag.

T-B: We got to do something about this Muslim in the Oval Office. Telling white men to eat their peas.

T-A: I took my Klan outfit from the attic trunk and sent it to the cleaners when I heard that. The nerve of that prissy nigger.

T-B: But at least we got respect from the media. Maybe they're not so liberal after all. Praising us.

T-A: Yea, Gloria Borger of CNN said that we stood by our principles and Michelle Cottle of *The Daily Beast* said that we were pure.

T-B: Even that commie paper *The New York Times* is kissing our butt. You see that guy Joe Nocera, apologizing for calling us terrorists?

T-A: Like a little punk assed bitch.

T-B: And that Mark Halperin.

T-A: Mark who?

T-B: You know the guy who was on Joe's show.

T-A: Oh, right. The guy who called coonskin a dick.

T-B: They suspended him and he came back the other day and was kissing the asses of both Rick Perry and our Tea Party. Said that we were "rational."

T-A: Incredible.

(*T-B orders another bottle. Black bartender brings one.*)

T-B- (*To bartender.*) Too bad about LeBron and Tiger, huh?

(*Nudges T-A. They grin. Bartender ignores them. Walks to the end of the bar and continues reading the* Washington Post.)

T-B: Yeah we don't care whether we get re-elected or not. We won't compromise. Tar Baby says he's for compromise. I got his compromise right here—(*Grabs his balls*). Boehner or none of these responsible conservatives (*sarcastically*) can't make us toe the line including that jackass McCain. Nobody owns us.

T-A: (*Ringtones: "Dixie"*) Hello… Oh Mr. Koch. It's so thrilling to hear from you… We almost got the default but these moderate…. I don't have to tell you? Thanks for being so understanding, Sir. Right. Right…. Thank you Sir.

T-B: The boss says he's flying us all out to the ranch to plan the next move. They're sending out an SOS about Wisconsin. Rove is going to show up. (*All choked up.*)

T-A: What's the matter? (*Puts his arm about T-B's shoulder.*)

T-B: He said that the Gipper would be proud of us. (*They embrace.*)

T-A: Let's get back to the family house. Grab the bottle.

(*They climb from the bar stools and begin to leave the bar. On the way out they run into Boehner and his entourage entering for Happy Hour.*)

Boehner: Oh, hi Congressman T-A, and T-B. We didn't get everything that we wanted but it was still a good deal, don't you think?

T-A: (*Pulls down his pants. Bends over, and issues a foul gaseous cloud toward the speaker, who with his entourage rushes into the bar. T-A and T-B can't stop laughing.*)

The End

PART II

"Coonery and Buffoonery"

The Selling of *Precious*[1]

"A niche market could be defined as a component that gives your business power. A niche market allows you to define whom you are marketing to. When you know who you are marketing to it's easy to determine where your marketing energy and dollars should be spent."

Defining Your Niche Market, A Critical Step in Small Business Marketing by Laura Lake

One can view Sarah Siegel on "YouTube" discussing her approach to marketing. During her dispassionate recital she says that she sees a "niche dilemma," and finds a way to solve that dilemma. Seeing that no one had supplied women with panties that were meant to be visible while wearing low cut jeans, she captured the niche and made a fortune. With five million dollars, she invested in the film *Precious,* which was adapted from the book *Push* written by Ramona Lofton, who goes by the pen name of Sapphire, after the emasculating shrew in *Amos and Andy,* a show created by white vaudevillians Freeman Gosden and Charles Correll.

(Ms. Lofton also knows a thing or two about marketing. Noticing the need for white New York feminists to use black men as the fall

---

1. A version of this article appeared at CounterPunch.org, Weekend Edition, December 4-6, 2009. It provoked a nation-wide debate that continued until the Academy Awards in March and after.

guys for world misogyny, while keeping silent about the misogyny of those who share their ethnic background, she joined in on the lynching of five black and Hispanic boys, "who grew up in jail" after the rape of a Central Park jogger. She made money, and became famous. The boys were innocent!)

When Lionsgate Studio and Harvey Weinstein were quarrelling over the rights to *Push*, which has been marketed under the title of *Precious*, about a pregnant 350-pound illiterate black teenager who has borne her father's child and is assaulted sexually by her mother, Sarah Greenberg, speaking for Lionsgate, said that the movie would provide the studio with "a gold mine of opportunity," which is probably true, since the image of the black male as sexual predator has created a profit center for over one hundred years and even won elections for politicians like Bush, The First.

But politicians, the KKK, Nazis, film, television, etc., had done the black male as a rapist to death. The problem for Sarah and Lionsgate and her film company Smokewood, was to solve "the niche dilemma," which they saw as selling a black film to white audiences (the people to whom CNN and MSNBC are referring to when they invoke the phrase "The American People.") An article in *The New York Times* (February 4, 2009) reported on the confusion among the investors as they fumbled about for a marketing plan.

> The studio prides itself on taking on marketing challenges, but *Push*,... is one of the biggest to come along in some time, marketing experts say. African-American audiences of all demographics could wince at the film's negative imagery. As films like *The Great Debaters* and *Miracle at St. Anna* have shown, a release labeled a black film by the marketplace—and *Push* already has been—can be an incredibly tough sell to mainstream white audiences.

> Lionsgate already seems a little befuddled. On Monday the company initially agreed to discuss the inherent marketing challenges. A few hours later it backtracked, rejecting any marketing talk but saying executives would be happy to speak broadly about their delight in nabbing the movie. Before long that offer was also rescinded.

Three standing ovations given at *Push*'s test run at Sundance convinced some of the business people that although white audiences might decline to support films that show cerebral blacks, *The Great Debaters*, in which Denzel Washington plays the great black poet Melvin Tolson, or Spike Lee's *Miracle at St. Anna*, which shows heroic blacks, they would probably enjoy a film in which blacks were shown as incestors and pedophiles. White audiences continuing to give the film standing ovations and prizes and critical acclaim indicates that when Lionsgate's co-presidents for theatrical marketing, Sarah Greenberg and Tim Palen said of *Precious*, "There is simply a gold mine of opportunity here," they were on the money. It was Geoffrey Gilmore, director of the Sundance Film Festival, who enhanced the sales potential by providing the marketers led by Ms. Siegel with another selling point. In an interview he said that *Push* might hit "a cultural chord" because of all the discussion about race prompted by the election of President Obama. It was after their cynical manipulative tying of a black president to their sleazy product that I wanted Sarah to change the name of her panty company from So Low to How Low.

Michael Savage, Rush Limbaugh, and Glenn Beck who engage in a sort of corny 1930s-styled racist rhetoric could learn from Sarah. At times they look as though they've lost their minds and are not pleasant to look at, while a manicured, buffed Sarah, who doesn't go lightly on the eye shadow, looks better. She is salmon colored and though middle-aged wears baby doll clothes and if you Google her name, Sarah Siegel, along with "images" you'll find her posing in photos some of which have blacks smooching her.

The blog *Gawker* (22 Nov. 09) points to the way Limbaugh, Beck and Savage have tried to associate Obama and his administration with rape imagery. Ain't they out of touch. Sarah Siegel has joined an innovative marketing plan that couples Obama's name with the most extreme of sexual crimes.

This woman, who hangs out with Hollywood stars and unlike Bill O'Reilly, an Irish American who has lost his way, knows that blacks are able to handle table utensils—she's dined with them—

might have invested in a movie that some are calling the worst depiction of black life yet done.

New York Press critic, Armond White, in a brilliant take down of the movie, compares it with *Birth of a Nation*. I would argue that this movie makes D.W. Griffith look like a progressive. Moreover, I've looked at a number of pictures that show how the Nazis depicted blacks and though Jewish and black men appear as sexual predators in many, I've never run across one in which minority men are shown as incest violators.

The black sexual predator is represented obsessively in the novel that inspired the bombing of the Oklahoma Federal building and the recent murder of three Pittsburgh policemen. But not even *The Turner Diaries*, by William Pierce, stigmatizes black men as violators of the incest taboo at a time when the black male unemployment rate is 25 percent in some cities, 50 percent in New York. It took Hollywood liberals and their pathetic black front people to do that. Is there a role that black actors won't perform? One that celebrity blacks won't lend their names to? (If the white Oscar judges perpetrate a cruel joke by awarding this film Oscars, will the black audience members stage a walk-out even though it might mean never working in that town again?) Indeed it was Oprah Winfrey's endorsement of the film that convinced the investors that they were on to a hot property.

The *Times* reports:

> A deal did not emerge for *Push* until about a week after the festival ended, with potential distributors balking over the price insisted upon by Cinetic Media, a New York marketing and sales company for independent film, according to two people with knowledge of how the deal came together but who were not authorized to speak publicly.
>
> A spokeswoman for Cinetic declined to comment, but bidders said Ms. Winfrey and Mr. Perry had been crucial to the deal's coming together.

Indeed, the business model for both the book, *Push*, by Sapphire, renamed *Precious* for the movie by Lionsgate, which beat Harvey Weinstein for the rights in court, was the black incest product, *The*

Color Purple, which has been recycled so many times that comedian Paul Mooney says that he anticipates a "Color Purple" on ice. But even that incest film doesn't go as far as *Precious,* which shows both mother and father engaged in a sexual assault on their daughter in graphic detail, Sarah Siegel's way of solving her "niche dilemma."

TheRoot is *The Washington Post's* black zine, among whose bosses is Jacob Weisberg—he says that he helped to launch it and has considerable influence, like deciding who gets hired and fired. The zine's black face is Henry Louis Gates, Jr. Since the beginning of the movie's run *TheRoot* has provided cover for *Precious* probably because Gates is tight with Oprah Winfrey and wrote a kiss up book about her. (Now that Joel Dreyfuss has taken over, *TheRoot* will quit being a shameless promoter of stupid NeoCon "tough love" ideology. He is a journalist with integrity.) *TheRoot's* support for the film is at odds with the furor that has erupted among blacks across the country about this film.

Famous journalists like Jack White and Dori Maynard of the Maynard Institute say that they, like thousands of blacks, won't even go see it. The whites who are behind this film didn't have a black audience in mind when they drew up the business strategy for the film. Their "niche audience" got their money's worth. The naked black-skinned man Carl of medium build who rapes a 350-pound daughter, who elsewhere in the film goes about flattening people with one punch, is little more than an animal. A vile prop. A person with no story and no humanity. Writer Cecil Brown said that Carl is the real victim of the movie during an interview with Aimee Allison, a KPFA interviewer who has brought points of view that up to now have been missing from the Pacifica Network.

Sarah's "niche audience" is well served. The white characters are altruistic types, there to help downtrodden black people and are among those who are to be admired. They're there to correct blacks when they make mistakes, like a white girl who shows up in a special education class out of nowhere to explain to the character Precious the difference between the word "insect" and "incest." This also follows the Nazi model. Aryans were idealized; hated minorities were degenerate.

According to this film, if you're a lucky black woman, a white man will rescue you from the clutches of evil black men, which is why white male critics are slobbering all over this film, giving it standing ovations and awards every day. Even white critics at hip places like *The Rolling Stone*, a place where Elvis gets credit for "changing American music." This reminded me of Alice Walker's appeal to white men to rescue black women, printed in a London newspaper and Steven Spielberg's comment that when he read *The Color Purple* all he could think of was rescuing Celie, the abused heroine (while he has yet to make a movie about the Celies among his ethnic group).

(*The Huffington Post*'s embrace of the film probably explains Arianna Huffington's continued scolding of the president. During the week of November 23, 2009, she called the president, who is one of the hardest working presidents in history, "lackadaisical," which, to black people, who know the dog whistles, means lazy. Shiftless.)

The movie says that if a white knight is not around to sweep you up, maybe a fantasy light-skinned boyfriend will do the job. The light-skinned literacy teacher, whom the camera favors, and a firm welfare worker of the same skin tone, played by Mariah Carey, who has welfare recipients at her mercy, are among the movie's positive characters, while black and brown skinned women are shown as petty, sullen, quick tempered and violent. They romp through the movie scowling and glaring at people and telling people things like "you ain't shit." This film includes the worst portrayal of black women I've ever seen, which makes *TheRoot* contributors'—young black women professors—endorsement of the film puzzling.

These are the types who are using the university curriculum to get even with their fathers and teach courses in black women's literature, but can't identify more than three. (The great novelist, the late Kristin Hunter Lattany, who was driven out of her college teaching job by a racist campaign [see her novel, *Breaking Away*] did not receive a single retrospective from these women.)

They don't seem to read criticism by black women either. During an endorsement of *Precious,* one of them, writing in *TheRoot,* repeated the canard that only black men opposed *The Color Purple,* when the book and the movie offended some of most prominent literary stars. Barbara Smith, Toni Morrison, Michele Wallace, and bell hooks, who described the film as "aversion therapy" for white women, are authors of scathing comments about the book and Steven Spielberg's interpretation. Trudier Harris, next to Joyce Joyce, the most prominent of black women critics, said that she discontinued criticizing the book after retaliations from the powerful white feminist academic lobby.

Haven't these *TheRoot* contributors read Walker's *Stepping Into The Same River Twice* where Walker herself objects to Spielberg's treatment of that book's incestor, Mr.? Indeed Walker, Tina Turner and bell hooks have observed that in the hands of white male producers, directors and scriptwriters, the black male characters in the texts of black women writers become even more sinister. *TheRoot* accompanied its brown nosing of the movie with a picture of Celie, played by Whoopie Goldberg (who said that what Polanski did to that child was not "rape, rape") holding a knife against Mr.'s neck. That scene doesn't appear in the book. Spielberg put that knife in Celie's hand. Henry Louis Gates, Jr., who has been appointed Commissar of African-American culture, said that those who criticized *The Color Purple* were "misguided." Was he referring to Morrison? Wallace? hooks?

I suspect that the whites who are behind *Precious* monkeyed around with the text as well. A film in which gays are superior to black male heterosexuals ("They don't rape. They don't sell crack.") Next to the whites, the male who treats Precious and her dysfunctional friends with the most understanding is John John, the gay male nurse. (Lee Daniels, the gay "director" of the film once ran a nursing business.) In this movie Caribbean Americans are smarter than black Americans.

Oprah Winfrey is listed as the "Executive Director," along with Tyler Perry, whose movie efforts have been described by writer

Thembi Ford as "coonery." This is the third black man as sexual predator and the second black incest film that Ms. Winfrey has either endorsed or performed in, yet, only a few titles by black male authors have been adopted by her book club. On Sunday, November 23, during a phone interview with Keifer Bonvillain, author of *Ruthless*, an inside look at the Oprah operation, I asked him about her embrace of the black male as a sexual predator trope. He wrote:

> Last year, I published *Ruthless*, (a true story based on conversations I had with Oprah Winfrey's office manager). The book detailed the unfair treatment African-American men received from Oprah Winfrey and the negative stereotypical images of African-American men that Oprah sent out in her films. The office manager also gave me a rare glance of Oprah Winfrey's private life.
>
> This was the first time one of Oprah Winfrey's employees spoke openly about her as they are prevented from doing so by strict confidentiality agreements. Oprah tried hard to block publication of the book. She and her attorney went so far as to have me arrested. The charges were dropped and the book was published.
>
> Since the publication of *Ruthless*, I noticed several profound changes in the way Oprah Winfrey is doing business.
>
> 1) Oprah produced *The Great Debaters*, which was the first film produced by Harpo Films (in my opinion) to not have negative stereotypical images of black men.
>
> 2) This season, JayZ became the first African-American rap artist to perform on the Oprah Winfrey Show.
>
> 3) This season Oprah's book club selection, *Say You're One of Them*, was written by a black man, Uwem Akpan. This was the first time in years a black man who is not one of Oprah's friends was featured in the book club.
>
> I was very encouraged by what I was seeing. Then came *Precious*! Like her addiction to food, Oprah does well for a little while but she just can't help herself.

Another reason that Ms. Winfrey supports the film is because she endorses the policy points the movie makes about welfare recipients. Precious is encouraged to take a job as home-care worker for

$2.00 per hour. Throughout the movie, poor women are guided to WorkFare. The movie almost becomes a commercial for the program. The policy message is that welfare recipients are black women who wish to avoid work, who use their time having sex with their daughters, watching television and dining on pig leavings. They don't intervene when their boyfriends rape their children (even the grandmother refuses to intervene). Oprah's attitude toward welfare recipients was described by Pat Gowens, editor of *Mother Warriors Voice*. She said that "Oprah Winfrey" is "someone who reinforces the U.S. war on the poor and unequivocally supports white male supremacy." She writes about what happened to welfare mothers who were invited to appear on her show after threatening to picket the TV megastar.

> For 30 minutes before the show, Oprah's cheerleader worked the audience into a frenzy of hatred against moms on welfare. When the show started, Welfare Warriors member Linda, an Italian American mom with three children, was sandwiched between two women who attacked and pitied her. The African American mom on her right claimed to have overcome her "sick dependence on welfare" and bragged about cheating on welfare and allegedly living like a queen. The white woman on her left was not a mom but had once received food stamps. Both women aggressively condemned Linda for receiving welfare. Throughout the show Oprah alternated between attacking Linda and allowing panel and audience members to attack her. Poor Linda had been prepared to discuss the economic realities of mother work, the failures of both the U.S. workforce and the child support system, and the Welfare Warriors' mission to create a Government Guaranteed Child Support program (Family Allowance) like those in Europe. But instead Linda was forced to defend her entire life, while Oprah repeatedly demanded, "How long have you been on welfare?"

> Later we complained to Oprah and her producer about the false promises they had used to lure us onto the show. (We had engaged in extensive negotiations prior to agreeing to appear. We said yes only after they agreed to discuss welfare reform, not our personal lives.) The producer shoved an Oprah cup (our pay) into our hands and pushed us out the door, angrily denying their treachery.

By the time we arrived home, we had received calls from moms on both coasts warning us about the promos Oprah was using to advertise her show: "They call themselves welfare warriors and they refuse to work. See Oprah at 4:00."

Well, as my great grandmother often said, "If you dig a ditch for someone, dig two." Kitty Kelley, winner of a PEN Oakland Award for censorship, published *Oprah: A Biography* (Crown 2010). Was it Oprah's ditch? The publication of this book is the real reason why Oprah quit her show. Kelley has never been sued for libel and her book about the Bush family was so hot (and useful) that the Bush Klan succeeded in shutting it down with the help of Bush 1st's golf caddy, NBC's Matt Lauer. Editors of *The New York Times Magazine* section hold the same position about welfare recipients as Oprah.

I stopped reading *The New York Times Magazine* years ago, weary of its parade of flesh-eating black cannibals, lazy and shiftless welfare mothers. (The *Times'* coverage of Africa could be written by Edgar Rice Burroughs.) It is a section of the newspaper where Daniel Moynihan is treated as some kind of Celtic god. This is the guy who accused unmarried black mothers of "speciation."

A book promoted by the magazine in which all of the crack addicts were black and in which one photo showed a black crack addict, a mother, fellating a john while a baby was strapped to her back even offended Brent Staples, a black member of the editorial board. That crack is a black drug, exclusively, is just another media hoax meant to entertain whites of the kind that dates to the very beginning of the American mass media.

So I wasn't surprised that the magazine section featured a spread about *Precious* featuring Gabourey Sidibe, the 350-pound actor in the title role, on the cover, certainly an act of black exploitation. However the interviewer, gossip writer Lynn Hirschberg, did perform a service by catching Lee Daniels, the "director" of *Precious* in a couple of exaggerations. In an effort to follow the marketing plan, the title of the article was "The Audacity of Precious," after Obama's "The Audacity of Hope" subtitled "Is America Ready For A Movie About An Obese Harlem Girl Raped And Impregnated By

Her Abusive Father?" Lionsgate spent big bucks to advertise the movie in *The Times*.

During Lynn Hirschberg's interview with Daniels, he claims that he directed *Monster's Ball*, about a black woman so dimwitted that she begins a relationship with her husband's white executioner (though as a porn movie it was superior to *Co-Ed Confidential*). The husband was played by Sean Puffy Combs.

Turns out that Daniels didn't direct the film. It was directed by Marc Forster, a white director. So, did Daniels direct *Precious* or is really he playing the flak catcher for this heinous project like Oprah Winfrey and Perry? When he went on the set to exercise his role as "director" did the white people who own the movie and provide the crew for this film call security? Hard to say. He also said that he grew up in the ghetto. His aunt disputes this.

The Times has printed no less than four articles all of which have either praised *Precious* or given those who defend the movie the most lines. Two were written by A.O. Scott, who said that this movie about fictional characters was part of a "national conversation about race." This is the problem with films like *Precious*. White critics like A.O. Scott, who hog all the criticism space as black, Hispanic, and Asian American journalists are being fired in droves, get a chance to pick and choose the cultural products that will ignite a discussion about race, usually ones that show blacks as depraved individuals, individuals that are used to blame black men and in this case black women, collectively. He suggests that based upon a movie adapted from a fiction, all black males are incest violators, the kind of group libel aimed at the brothers when Gloria Steinem said that *The Color Purple* told the truth about black men.

Why didn't *Dexter, Paris Trout* or Dorothy Allison's *Bastard Out Of Carolina* begin "a national conversation," about race? Ted Turner tried to suppress *Bastard Out Of Carolina*, this white incest film and only through the intervention of Anjelica Huston was the film aired. Turner pronounced it too graphic to be shown on his network CNN, which poses blacks as degenerates 24/7. In several states, *Bastard* has been banned from classrooms and school libraries.

Also, why doesn't the *Times* open its Jim Crow Op-Ed page so that a member of *Precious*'s target, black men, as a class, could respond to this smear, this hate crime as entertainment, this neo-Nazi porn and filth? There are hundreds of black male intellectuals (yes, black men are more than athletes, criminals and entertainers) who would take up the challenge. But the Op-Ed page is only open to one black writer, consistently—Orlando Patterson— who, like the '20s writer Claude McKay, is the kind of Jamaican who has nothing but contempt for African Americans.

Sapphire (Ramona Lofton), who wrote the novel *Push,* also has a biography like Daniels' that shifts about. First she told Dinitia Smith of the *Times* (July 2, 1996) that Precious was an actual person. "She lives there," she said, "pointing at a dowdy building over a check-cashing store." Don't you think that if such a person existed that Lionsgate wouldn't include her in its marketing plan so ubiquitous that an ad for this film appears on my email screen when I sign in at AOL. It figures. AOL's expert on black culture and politics is Dinesh D'Souza. Their coverage of black culture is limited to black NFL and NBA athletes who get into trouble outside of strip clubs.

Part of the packaging of both the novel and the film has been to cash in on the culture of recovery. Sapphire says that she was a former prostitute and a victim of incest (Lee Daniels does his pity party routine during the *Times*' interview). She also said that she is a recovering lesbian. In 1986, she began to "remember things." "An incident of violent sexual abuse" when she was "3 or 4." Her father, an Army sergeant, denied her claim. He died in 1990. (Lee Daniels also "remembered" abuse by his father. I wonder what his aunt would say.)

Her "remembering things" and being inspired by two other profitable black incest products led Alfred Knopf to give her a $500,000 advance for two books, one of which, entitled *American Dreams,* included a poem called "Wild Thing," which blamed the rape of a Central Park jogger on black boys.

As Steven Spielberg put the knife in Celie's hand, Sapphire put a rock and pipe into the hands of boys who spent their youth in jail for a crime that they didn't commit. She has her narrator say: "I bring the rock down/on her head/sounds dull & flat/like the time I busted/the kitten's head/the blood is real and red/my dick rises." She has one of the defendants, Yusef Salaam, participating in the rape. "Yosef slams her/across the face with a pipe." Yusef Salaam served five and half years. Do you think that Sapphire might make up to Mr. Salaam for destroying his reputation in a book for which she received $500,000? And what about Naomi Wolfe and other millionaire feminists whose agitation helped to convict these innocent kids? Maybe they can join Sapphire in setting up a trust fund for these victims "who grew up in jail." And what about Linda Fairstein? She got rich, too.

Called a "Zealot, Crusader, and Megalomaniac," Linda Fairstein, of the Manhattan District Attorney's Sex Crimes Unit, often shown as an "ultra-blond" in an "air-brushed" photo, saw prosecuting these children as a step toward fame and fortune. In the words of Rivka Gewirtz Little, author of "Ash-Blond Ambition, Prosecutor Linda Fairstein May Have Tried Too Hard" (*Village Voice*, 19 November 2002), they were convicted as a result of the zealousness of the ambitious prosecutor, the Jim Crow media (which found them guilty and contributed to the hysteria surrounding the case) and by New York feminists, black and white. (Donald Trump wanted the children to get the death penalty.) Little writes: "The men in all of these cases, who were convicted despite the existence of exculpatory evidence, still see Fairstein and her minions as either zealots or headline seekers, pursuing verdicts that would appease the outraged public. Oliver Jovanovic thinks Fairstein was also making literary hay from her cases."

Jovanovic, "the Columbia University microbiology Ph.D. candidate, dubbed the 'cybersex' attacker, who was convicted and sentenced to 15 years to life in prison for kidnapping and sexually torturing a Barnard undergraduate," also had his own run-in with Fairstein. Little continued: "After he served nearly two years of his prison term, an appeals court overturned his conviction in 1999, again saying that crucial evidence was withheld during the trial that

could have shown Jovanovic and his accuser had a consensual sado-
masochistic relationship, or that she simply fabricated the story.
Morgenthau dismissed the case before a pending retrial in 2001. (…)
'Each time one of these cases occurred, her books probably went
flying off the shelves,' says Jovanovic. 'She used what happened in
that unit to make money, and that is wrong.' (…) she earned, according to *The New York Times*, $2.5 million in sales by 1999."

Little also questioned the rush to judgment of feminists in the
case in her, "How Feminists Faltered on the Central Park Jogger
Case" (*Village Voice*, October 15, 2002).

> Feminists who rallied on the courthouse stairs outside the 1990 trial of
> five African American and Latino youth accused in the infamous rape
> and beating of the 28-year-old Central Park jogger made it painfully
> clear—there was a choice to make: gender or race. With flimsy evidence
> and an almost immediate indictment by the public, advocates for the
> teens believed they were easy lynch victims and demanded further
> investigation and fair trials. But to some feminists, bringing up 'the
> race issue' muddled the case and detracted from the bottom-line issue—
> violence against women and justice for the victim.
>
> Thirteen years after the teens were convicted, DNA evidence and a
> confession to the crime by Matias Reyes, a convicted rapist behind bars,
> indicate a strong possibility that the five accused—who walked into
> prison as boys and emerged years later as men—would have been a
> worthy cause for any left activist group to champion. In the jogger case,
> no one even considered their five mothers a cause for feminists, though
> with little money or proper representation, they saw their sons rail-
> roaded, and the media portrayed them as out-of-control ghetto mamas.

The young men, who went to prison as children, Antron McCray,
Kevin Richardson, Raymond Santana, Kharey Wise, and Yusef
Salaam, received from five and a half to thirteen years.

Because of his defense of the poem "Wild Thing" by Sapphire
(Ramona Lofton), printed in a literary journal, the *Portable Lower
East Side*, which "was a graphic depiction of the thoughts of a par-
ticipant in the rape and beating of a Central Park jogger," according
to *The Washington Post*, John Frohnmayer was fired as head of the
National Endowment of the Arts. During an appearance before the

National Press Club, he warned that "the political battle over the NEA [was] part of a broader cultural war and invoked the specter of the Nazis' takeover of Europe to underscore his point." Another technique the Nazis used, whether Frohnmayer knows it, was to blame their enemies for crimes they didn't commit like the burning of the Reichstag, which is what happened in the Central Park case. The "wilders," it turned out, were innocent. When Little called to ask feminists who judged the children guilty, when no forensic evidence tied them to the rape, and after Matias Reyes confessed to the crime (his semen matched that collected from the jogger), only one would respond. Susan Brownmiller, who libeled all black men as rapists in her book *Against Our Will*, was a holdout.

She said that regardless of the scientific evidence pointing away from the guilt of the five, she still believed that they were guilty. I wonder, was Sapphire called? I wonder how she feels about her poem. I wonder whether we would have found out if Katie Couric had given her the kind of grilling that she gave Sarah Palin. One of the reasons that Bryant Gumbel left NBC was that Couric was chosen to interview O.J. Simpson instead of him.

Sapphire, who helped to set up these children, the way that she and her cynical backers like Sarah Siegel, whose depiction of black men is worse than those found in *American Renaissance* magazine, have set up black men. In *Precious,* the out-of-control ghetto mama whom they market is played by Mo'Nique. Carl, her husband, who commits the unspeakable, is Sapphire and Sarah Siegel's "Wild Thing."

I asked D. Scott Miller, a writer for the *San Francisco Bay Guardian*, his take on the different biographies of Ramona Lofton. He said,

> I would say that her bio has been shortened and extended when it's convenient. Here's the opening of her Amazon Bio:
>
> "Sapphire was born in 1950 and spent her first twelve years on Army bases in California and Texas. As a teenager she lived in South Philadelphia and Los Angeles. She graduated from City College in New York and received an MFA from Brooklyn College. From 1983 to 1993

she lived in Harlem, where she taught reading and writing to teenagers and adults. She lives in New York City."

Here's the opening of her bio post-*Push*, but pre-*Precious*:

"Ramona Lofton, better known to her readers as Sapphire, was born in 1950 in Fort Ord, California. On the surface, her family was characterized as normal and middle class. Her father was an Army sergeant and her mother was a member of the Women's Army Corps. As a child, Sapphire's family relocated several time to various cities, states, and countries. When she was only 13 years old, Sapphire's mother became the victim of alcoholism and eventually departed from her life. Her mother died in 1983. In that same year, her brother, who was then homeless was killed in a public park."

I would not say that she is lying, or even stretching the truth. But I see a difference. Don't know which one she's using right now.

I wasn't surprised that NPR's Terry Gross would become part of the film's promotion. I stopped listening to her years ago because she seemed to have a thing about casting all black men as sexual predators.

She once maneuvered a famous black writer into directing her wrath against her father toward all black men and when a woman from South Africa was brought on to discuss the rapes occurring in that country, Gross asked whether rape in that country was interracial. The woman answered that white men rape too, which seemed to come as a surprise to Ms. Gross. When whatever is bothering Ms. Gross about black men gains entry in *The Diagnostic and Statistical Manual of Mental Disorders*, maybe the editors will name it after her. Gross's Syndrome. Or maybe she and Ms. Brownmiller can flip a coin.

I only tuned into Ms. Gross's interview with Daniels because poet Al Young called and asked me to do so. It was instructive. The NPR airwaves were full of giggles as they carried on their dialogue. At one point, she asked whether violence among blacks is cultural. He said that it was hereditary, thereby signing on to about two centuries of quack race "science" and a neo-Nazi line promoted by *The Times*' Sam Roberts who once wrote that blacks were "prone" to violence and by the Op-Ed pages' token black contributor, Orlando Patterson, who wrote recently as though violence is black.

This in a country where the National Rifle Association owns or intimidates every politician but Michael Bloomberg; where one hundred million guns are available and where accidental deaths by gunshots in white homes dwarf those occurring in the inner city, which is not to excuse such deaths, which lead to high homicide rates.

One of the reasons is that the police, white and suburban, have a poor record of solving urban crimes and as a result of NAFTA, thousands have joined the underground economy (in Oakland, where I live, only 37 percent of homicides are solved; in nearby Danville, an affluent city, when a white youth's murder resulted from a drug transaction gone wrong, eleven detectives were assigned to the case, and the killer was caught the next day).

Daniels' and Gross's discussion about the black violence gene occurred at a time when the National Association of Black Journalists was criticizing NPR for its firing of black personnel. And so when *The Times* and the producers of *Precious* are profiting from stereotypes that reach back to the Enlightenment, they receive an endorsement from NPR whose "Ghetto 101," produced by the late Ellen Willis, was one of the most offensive of black pathology ratings boosters and money makers. Violence?

The white majority has given mandates to policies that have resulted in the murders of millions of people since World War II.

While white male critics are campaigning feverishly to land one or two Oscars for *Precious,* the dissent from some black critics has been blistering. Most notably Armond White who, as a result of his review printed in *The New York Press* has become a folk hero among young black cyberspace intellectuals of the kind who are making a comeback after about twenty years of the left and right establishments laying black intellectuals on us who sing from the same songbook as they. One of those who praised White's review printed in *The New York Press*, was Kofi Natambu, the brilliant young editor of *The Panopticon Review.* I asked him what he thought was behind *Precious*:

The withering contempt and sheer malice for black people (and especially black men) that this film represents and embodies is an integral part of a very disturbing and destructive trend among a number of cultural hustlers, thieves, and conmen and women in film, literature, theatre, and the music industry that is being vigorously promoted and marketed by white corporations and Madison Avenue. It's no coincidence that the increasingly casual and overt racism that is routinely displayed in advertising and the media generally is working hand in glove with the contemptible and venal likes of artistic pimps and prostitutes like Lee Daniels, Tyler Perry, and Oprah Winfrey. This development has been dismissing, marginalizing, and destroying the impact and influence of genuine African-American artists in all the arts now since the mid '90s and has in the past decade reached its vicious apex in the heinous "work" of such black retrograde and reactionary assholes as the people producing and directing this film. Remember Percival Everett's brilliant novel from 2001 called *Erasure*? Remember his devastating critique of this nexus of white racism and black minstrel confidence schemes in his rendering of the phony black author (who sounds a LOT like Sapphire!) called *My Pafology*? as now this is what this ugly marriage between the white corporate media and Uncle Tom/Aunt Thomasina minstrelism has come to in the modern world. If something is not done to stem this tide it's only going to get worse and soon.

My Pafology indeed.

Armond White wrote:

Winfrey, Perry and Daniels make an unholy triumvirate. They come together at some intersection of race exploitation and opportunism. These two media titans—plus one shrewd pathology pimp—use *Precious* to rework Booker T. Washington's early 20th-century manifesto *Up From Slavery* into extreme drama for the new millennium: Up From Incest, Child Abuse, Teenage Pregnancy, Poverty and AIDS. Regardless of its narrative details about class and gender, *Precious* is an orgy of prurience. All the terrible, depressing (not uplifting) things that happen to 16-year-old Precious recall that memorable "All About Eve" line, "Everything but the bloodhounds nipping at her rear-end.

As a result of his dissent A.O. Scott dismissed Armond White as "a contrarian" which means that his conclusions about the film differed from those of white critics. Novelist Diane Johnson had it right when she pointed out, sagaciously, in *The New York Times Magazine*, that many whites engage in a perverse voyeurism when viewing black culture.

They want to peek behind the curtains of black life to seek confirmation that all of the myths they've heard about black life are true. Richard Wright said that, "the Negro is America's metaphor." More like America's anti-depressant. People who are miserable in their own lives are getting off by consuming black depravity, a big business. The audience at the 2 o'clock matinee that I attended was 90 percent white, the marketer's "niche" audience. Not only did I have to swallow this seedy material to possibly enter this review in my book, *Barack Obama and the Jim Crow Media, The Return of the Nigger Breakers* (Baraka Books, 2010), but was assaulted by two offensive previews: Clint Eastwood's movie about Nelson Mandela and Disney's *The Princess and the Frog*, a black Princess this time, which, judging from the trailers, will be a remake of *Song of the South*. In the film, Iku ("*eniti ile re mbe lagbedemeji aiye on orun*" or "the entity that stands between heaven and earth"), the top-hatted mythological figure from the Yoruba religion is depicted as evil (in the film he is Doctor Facilier, "a schemer, a conjurer and a sorcerer of sorts"), and a follower of Oshun, a water spirit, with thousands of followers in this hemisphere, is caricatured in the movie. In the movie her name is Mama Odie. It's bad enough that Oprah endorses the stupid and mindless *Precious* but then she has to go perform for Disney. A project that demeans African religion. And has already been criticized by some blacks for the black Princess lacking a black male love interest. *The Daily Mail* reported on March 18, 2009.

> With America's first African-American president in the White House, Disney is counting on an African-American princess to be a big hit in Hollywood. But even though "The Princess and the Frog" isn't released until later this year, it is already stirring up controversy. For while Princess Tiana and many in the cartoon cast are black—the prince is not. Which has led some critics to complain that Disney has ducked the opportunity for a fairytale ending for a black prince and princess.

Both directors and all of the screenwriters for this movie are white
men. I recommend that they and Oprah read William Bascom's
Sixteen Cowries, Yoruba Divination From Africa To The New World.

This kind of ridiculing of black culture is nothing new for Disney.
In a 1932 cartoon Mickey and Minnie were pitted against "fierce
niggers."

The opinions of black moviegoers about *Precious* probably concur
with those of White and Courtland Milloy. The latter, from *The
Washington Post,* wrote: "I watched the movie at a theater in
Alexandria where show times are nearly around the clock, from 10:15
a.m. to 12:15 a.m. The audience was mostly black women and teenagers. When the lights came up, all of the moviegoers appeared sullen and depressed that I attended." Milloy continued: "After escaping
the abuse of her home life, Precious ends up in a halfway house. She
is still functionally illiterate and has two babies to care for, one with
Down syndrome. Strangest of all, many reviewers felt the movie
ended on a high note. *Time,* for instance, wrote that Precious 'makes
an utterly believable and electrifying rise from an urban abyss of
ignorance and neglect.' Excuse me, the movie ends with the girl
walking the streets, babies in her arms, having just learned that her
father has died of AIDS — but not before infecting her."

As a weak justification, and following the prompting of Geoffrey
Gilmore, Lee Daniels told *The Times* interviewer that he was mind-
ful that the movie contained stereotypes but that was okay because
we have a black president, which must thrill the birthers, the tea
baggers, those who create posters in which Obama appears as witchdoctor, a Muslim and the joker. On November 23, 2009, some wing-
nut put up a picture of Michelle Obama as a monkey at Goggle. The
haters of the Obamas must really feel in vogue thanks to Daniels.

Another part of the pitch is that the men in the film could be men
of any ethnic group, a sales pitch used by Pulitzer Prize winner Lynn
Nottage for her theatrical products, praised by some of the same
types who are crazy about *Precious. Atlanta Constitution* columnist
Cynthia Tucker received a Pulitzer for referring to black men as
"idle" and "bestial" and they awarded Janet Cooke one for making

up a story about black parents who were so rotten that they made heroin available to an eight year old, over the objection of a black panelist who smelled a fraud. Three great playwrights, Adrienne Kennedy, Ed Bullins and Amiri Baraka, have never received a Pulitzer. These black men on the screen or on the stage doing terrible things to women could be Bosnians so the line goes.

In her interview with Daniels, Lynn Hirschberg said something similar: "Precious is a stand-in for anyone—black, white, male, female—who has ever been devalued or underestimated."

To which Milloy answered:

> Let's see: I lose my job, so I take in a movie about a serially abused black girl and I go, "Oh, swell, she's standing in for me." Maybe there is something to the notion that when human pathology is given a black face, white people don't have to feel so bad about their own. At least somebody's happy. Sexual abuse is certainly an equal-opportunity crime, with black and white women similarly affected. But only exaggerated black depravity seems to resonate so forcefully in the imagination.

Will the "niche" audience for which this movie is intended ever become weary of the brothers being symbols of universal male misogyny? Or the face on the bull's-eye at which disgruntled feminists from all ethnic groups aim their arrows, while women are scared to challenge the misogyny practiced by males who share their background? Judging from the box office receipts, maybe not. As of November 22, 2009, three weeks after the film's debut, box office receipts totaled a gross of $21,277,521.

What is the solution offered by the people behind this film for the millions of blacks who are suffering from a depression during white America's recession? After a hurried flurry of images belonging to Malcolm X, Martin Luther King, Jr. and Shirley Chisholm, *Precious* becomes redeemed by semi-literacy and black pride. The film's true ending occurs when Precious and her mother engage in a furious battle; the black pride part seems forced. After the mother/daughter battle, the movie lingers like a wounded animal that nobody has the nerve to put out of its misery. Even more dreadful was somebody's idea to tack on one of these trite sistuh solidarity songs.

What else do the film makers recommend that the underclass do, people who in the movie go into stores and rob and down a whole bucket of fried chicken, an image borrowed from *The Birth of a Nation*? Go to church and get sterilized which is the subtle Eugenics message that appears on a sign, "Spay and Neuter Your Pets," as Precious and her two children travel to their new apartment.

According to Stefan Kuhl in his book, *The Nazi Connection, Eugenics, American Racism and German National Socialism*, sterilization is an idea that the Germans borrowed from the United States as a way of ending the reproduction of unwanted groups. People who possess a violence gene?

In the mid-seventies, the late Chester Himes predicted that the Establishment was trying to start a war between black men and women. They succeed by treating both groups as opposing sports teams. And so while Armond White has been denounced by defenders of the movie, many of them women, and whites who consider him a "contrarian," the woman who put up the money, Sarah Siegel, has chosen to remain in the background. None of the exchanges I've read even mention her name. (Nor do they mention the names of those who made up the executive leadership of the company, Lionsgate, that produced the film. All white males, reminding us that the majority of black bogeyman films are produced, directed or are the results of scripts written by white males.) While the print and blog war over *Precious* rages on, she relaxes in her mansion, counting the profits from her 'Gold Mine of Opportunity': *Precious*; which is to blacks what Mel Gibson's *The Passion of Christ* was to Jews.

Finally, who will market the next black movie that white audiences will pay to see? MSNBC has been drawing a lot of laughs from the same demographic by running a story about a black man who has been arrested twice for having intercourse with a horse and infecting the horse. Even the token progressives on MSNBC favor this story. I'll bet somebody is working on the screenplay and the niche marketing for the film. Sarah, you listening?

Fade to White[1]

Judging from the mail I've received, the conversations I've had and all that I've read, the responses to "*Precious*: Based on the Novel '*Push*' by Sapphire" fall largely along racial lines.

Among black men and women, there is widespread revulsion and anger over the Oscar-nominated film about an illiterate, obese black teenager who has two children by her father. The author Jill Nelson wrote: "I don't eat at the table of self-hatred, inferiority or victimization. I haven't bought into notions of rampant black pathology or embraced the overwrought, dishonest and black-people-hating pseudo-analysis too often passing as post-racial cold hard truths." One black radio broadcaster said that he felt under psychological assault for two hours. So did I.

The blacks who are enraged by *Precious* have probably figured out that this film wasn't meant for them. It was the enthusiastic response from white audiences and critics that culminated in the film being nominated for six Oscars by the Academy of Motion Picture Arts and Sciences, an outfit whose 43 governors are all white and whose membership in terms of diversity is about 40 years behind Mississippi. In fact, the director, Lee Daniels, said that the honor would bring even more "middle-class white Americans" to his film.

Is the enthusiasm of such white audiences and awards committees based on their being comfortable with the stereotypes shown?

1. A version of this article appeared as an Op-Ed in *The New York Times* on February 4, 2010.

Barbara Bush, the former first lady, not only hosted a screening of *Precious* but also wrote about it in *Newsweek*, saying: "There are kids like Precious everywhere. Each day we walk by them: young boys and girls whose home lives are dark secrets." Oprah Winfrey, whose endorsement assisted the movie's distribution and its acceptance among her white fanbase, said, "None of us who sees the movie can now walk through the world and allow the Preciouses of the world to be invisible."

Are Mrs. Bush and Ms. Winfrey suggesting, on the basis of a fictional film, that incest is widespread among black families? Statistics tell us that it's certainly no more prevalent among blacks than whites. The National Center for Victims of Crime notes: "Incest does not discriminate. It happens in families that are financially privileged, as well as those of low socio-economic status. It happens to those of all racial and ethnic descent, and to those of all religious traditions."

Given the news media's tendency to use scandals involving black men, both fictional and real, to create "teaching tools" about the treatment of women, it was inevitable that a black male character associated with incest would be used to begin some national discussion about the state of black families.

This use of movies and books to cast collective shame upon an entire community doesn't happen with works about white dysfunctional families. It wasn't done, for instance, with *Requiem for a Dream*, starring the great Ellen Burstyn, about a white family dealing with drug addiction, or with *The Kiss*, a memoir about incest—in that case, a relationship between a white father and his adult daughter.

Such stereotyping has led to calamities being visited on minority communities. I've suggested that the Newseum in Washington create a Hall of Shame, which would include the front pages of newspapers whose inflammatory coverage led to explosions of racial hatred. I'm thinking, among many others, of 1921's Tulsa riot, which started with a rumor that a black man had assaulted a white woman, and resulted in the murder of 300 blacks.

Black films looking to attract white audiences flatter them with another kind of stereotype: the merciful slave master. In guilt-free bits of merchandise like *Precious,* white characters are always portrayed as caring. There to help. Never shown as contributing to the oppression of African Americans. Problems that members of the black underclass encounter are a result of their culture, their lack of personal responsibility.

It's no surprise either that white critics—eight out of the nine comments used on the publicity Web site for *Precious* were from white men and women—maintain that the movie is worthwhile because, through the efforts of a teacher, this girl begins her first awkward efforts at writing.

Redemption through learning the ways of white culture is an old Hollywood theme. D. W. Griffith produced a series of movies in which Chinese, Indians and blacks were lifted from savagery through assimilation. A more recent example of climbing out of the ghetto through assimilation is *Dangerous Minds,* where black and Latino students are rescued by a curriculum that doesn't include a single black or Latino writer.

By the movie's end, Precious may be pushing toward literacy. But she is jobless, saddled with two children, one of whom has Down syndrome, and she's learned that she has AIDS.

Some redemption.

The NAACP House of Shame[1]

"I think he's mentally ill. He's lost it. It's like he's departed from being a creative artist to being a basher. ... He's a forgotten man, eclipsed by women ascending to new heights and getting prizes. Instead of applauding them, he goes on a rampage."
– Sapphire on Ishmael Reed's state of mind, *The St. Louis Post Dispatch*, February 28, 2010

Suppose the producers of a nominated picture like *Hurt Locker* donated one million dollars to the Academy of Motion Picture Arts and Sciences, and on the night of the Oscar presentations *Hurt Locker* received Oscars for best picture, best actress, best supporting actress and a special honor was awarded to the "producer."

This is exactly what happened at the NAACP Image awards on February 26, 2010. The film *Precious* received six awards as a kind of payback to Tyler Perry who donated one million plus dollars to the organization last November.

As a result, the NAACP gave segregated Hollywood the green light to admire this abhorrent, repellant movie. They must be gloating over at *EW.com* (*Entertainment Weekly*) sites with connections to the Oscars establishment and where my Op-Ed about *Precious* printed in *The New York Times* was the subject of criticism by Owen Gleiberman and Lisa Schwarzbaum. Their criticism was picked up by Sasha Stone at *awardsdaily.com*. They and the bloggers who weighed in about my state of mind and my low I.Q. and how I was

---

1. A version of this article appeared at Counterpunch.org on March 5, 2010.

connected to the part of the body that plays a key role in the elimination of wastes will probably use these NAACP awards as justification for their defense of the film and as evidence of the black community's support for *Precious.*

Owen Gleiberman, a man whom I have never met, said that my criticism of the movie said more about me than about the movie. He never said what my criticism of the movie said about me. I also challenged Ms. Schwarzbaum to comment about an article printed in a Jewish magazine, *Tablet* ("Gentlemen Prefer Blondes, Why Jewish Producers Kept Jewish Women Off Stage and Screen," 20 October 2009), which pointed to the discrimination against Jewish women by Jewish producers, from the early days of Hollywood to the period of Woody Allen and Larry David (a guy who thinks it funny to appear in a scene eating a cookie shaped like a black penis).

The producers' justification, historically, was that they didn't want their women to play the kind of roles they assigned to black and white gentile women.

Ms. Schwarzbaum didn't answer, but seems satisfied with the roles assigned to black women in *Precious,* which now bears the imprimatur of the NAACP, the nation's leading civil rights organization. On March 2, when I debated Cameron Bailey, the African American co-director of the Toronto Film Festival, who brought the film to Canada, the NAACP awards were the first thing that he brought up. He also followed the sales pitch directed by Lionsgate that the critics of the film were either odd or mentally ill, as a way of minimizing the widespread discontent about this film among black Americans. The sales office has singled out Armond White as the lone critic opposing the film, and seeks to dismiss him as a "contrarian," a trend begun by *The New York Times'* critic A.O. Scott, for whom the family in *Precious* was the typical impoverished black family. Bailey used the same word to criticize White.

Now, Bailey and the critics at *EW,* including amateur shrink Owen Gleiberman, and Sasha Stone would probably be outraged by a white producer receiving awards from an organization of which he is a benefactor, but will probably ignore or even seek to justify the million dollars plus donation that Tyler Perry, producer of *Precious,* gave to the NAACP in November.

Now if I am mentally ill for criticizing this film as Sapphire suggests, then I'm lucky to be spared the kind of racism that black mental patients experience. I've examined the kind of treatment accorded the poor and the black, the kind of people who are treated like trash by city governments, the kind of people who are experimented upon by the pharmaceutical companies, while white middle class patients receive talk therapy. Black kids are treated with toxic anti-depressant drugs even when it's not necessary, a clear case of behavior modification. I had enough creative ability remaining to stage a play, called *Body Parts,* about the exploitation of African Americans and Africans by rogue pharmaceutical companies that distribute drugs with full knowledge of harmful results. Paying stiff fines is just the cost of doing business. In this play and others I, with the help of Berkeley's Black Repertory Theater and The Nuyorican Poets Café, have created roles that challenge black actors and actresses, instead of degrading them with cliché roles as male sexual predators, prostitutes and women who marry their husband's executioner.

Cecil Brown and I produced the movie *Two Fer* about conflicts on a college campus, which like *The Great Debaters* and *Miracle at Saint Anna* isn't likely to wow a crossover audience. Spike Lee's *The Miracle at Saint Anna* was praised at a reception I attended which honored those Buffalo Soldiers who liberated Italian towns and cities during World War II.

It was held on February 12, at the San Francisco Presidio, where the audience viewed the movie *Inside Buffalo.* The black soldiers received honors from the Italians years before honors came for them during the Clinton administration. They were commanded by Southern officers because they were said to know how to handle Niggers and were often sent to the front without adequate ammunition. It was Spike Lee who brought this story to the screen instead of Tom Hanks, Clint Eastwood and Steven Spielberg, who can do "Mr." (in *The Color Purple*) but can't find space in his war movies for Ivan J. Houston, a Buffalo Soldier, author of the book, *Black*

Warriors, The Buffalo Soldiers of World War II. When is the last time you saw black soldiers enacting heroic deeds in a film?

Some of those at the reception, attended by over four hundred Italians, Italian Americans and others wept when an official from the Italian consulate told the black soldiers, "We will never forget."

In Oakland, the theater that presented *Miracle at Saint Anna* offered only one showing at 10:30 p.m. *Saint Anna* was eclipsed by *Precious.*

Sapphire charges that I have been eclipsed by black women authors, many of whom I was the first to publish. She says that I have been left behind with no prizes. That may be true, but the same can't be said about some of the prominent black women intellectuals and authors who have been offended by Sarah Siegel's movie. One of the black women writers whom I published when she was a student is Terry McMillan. Al Young and I were also the first to publish an excerpt from Ntozake Shange's *Colored Girls....* I introduced the poetry of the late Lucille Clifton to Langston Hughes who published her in a major anthology for the first time. (If an "old"—the adjective used by some of the young black womanist defenders of the film to describe me—loser like me can manage to publish the works of over thirty black women writers from the U.S. and Africa over the last five years, why can't Sapphire do the same and shouldn't she avoid verbs like "rampaging" in light of her poem "Wild Thing" which helped create the hysteria that resulted in five black and Hispanic kids being sent to prison for a crime that they didn't commit?)

During a recent interview that I conducted with Terry McMillan, the most popular of African-American women writers, she was fuming as she said that the film "went too far." (See p. 187.) Sapphire might dismiss me as mentally ill and jealous of black women who have eclipsed me and left me without prizes, but what is her answer to Ms. McMillan who is certainly not hurting for book sales, or Princeton Professor Melissa Harris-Lacewell? Is she crazy? Does her criticism of *Precious* say more about her than about the movie? She wrote "Undoubtedly Mo'Nique has given an amazing performance in *Precious*. But the critical and popular embrace of this depiction of a monstrous black mother has potentially important, and troubling, political meaning."

Apparently Gabourey Sidibe's mother Alice Tan Ridley also has problems with the film. My response to my critic Sasha Stone and the mob of hateful furious bloggers she raised at *awardsdaily.com* was that during one of her shopping sprees in Paris she might buy some gifts for Ms. Ridley. She's the real heroine of this whole sorry business. Ms. Ridley was offered a role in the movie but after reading the novel *Push,* turned it down. She'd rather earn her keep by singing in the New York subway than perform in *Precious.*

When I informed the hateful bloggers at *awardsdaily.com* of this fact they said that I'd made it up, but when I referred them to YouTube, where she belts out a stirring rendition of "What's Love Got To Do With It," they thought it cruel of me to direct them to the video. They are part of a nation of junkies, and *Precious* has become a sort of non-prescription drug for them. A cheap high. Some of those whites who defended the film against my criticisms admitted that they hadn't even seen it and I'm suffering from mental illness? Now the NAACP award will provide them with more psychological methadone. It will give the all-white Oscars' Board of Governors (37 men, 6 women) an excuse to salute this evil wretched thing, whose reward by the NAACP shows the sad decline of Julian Bond, who, when a young man, had a future so bright that he was considered for a vice presidential nomination. (Vice President of the Board of Governors is Kathleen Kennedy, who gave us *The Color Purple*. This means that *Precious* is a shoo-in for one of two Oscars.)

On Friday night, Julian Bond, the outgoing president of an organization that has been fighting stereotypes since 1915, shared the stage with a serial stereotypes trafficker and union buster, Tyler Perry, whose movie efforts were summed up by Spike Lee, the director of at least three movie classics as: "coonery and buffoonery."

In *The New York Times*, Charles Blow, in a column called "Tyler Perry's Crack Mother," challenged the repeated use of the black crack mother image by the filmmaker. He cited a 2007 study of college undergraduates published in the *Journal of Ethnicity and Substance Abuse* which found that young blacks' rates of illicit drug use was substantially lower than their counterparts, with black women having the lowest rates of all. Yet Owen Gleiberman says that the movie reflects reality. One of the awards ceremony's guests was Quentin Tarantino, whose movie *Pulp Fiction* was full of lame and goofy racist jokes and memorable lines like:

> Jimmie: When you came pullin' in here, did you notice a sign on the front of my house that said 'Dead Nigger Storage?'
>
> Jules: Jimmie, you know I ain't seen no shit......

Why was Julian Bond looking so grim during the ceremonies? He has a sense of history. He knows that the NAACP was not founded by minstrels but by intellectuals. They fought *The Birth of a Nation* and *Gone with the Wind*. Walter White, then NAACP's secretary, went to Hollywood in 1942 and protested the roles in which black actors were cast. One of his allies was ex-presidential candidate, Wendell Willkie, who, during a speech delivered at a luncheon for Hollywood bigwigs at 20th Century Fox, said: "... that many of the persons responsible for Hollywood films belong to a racial and religious group which had been a target of Hitler, and that they should be the last to be guilty of doing to another minority the things which had been done to them."

White "urged Hollywood to have courage enough to shake off its fears and taboos and to depict the Negro in films as a normal human being and an integral part of the life of America and the world." Walter White was opposed by those actors who benefited from stereotypical roles that in hindsight seem benign in light of the kind of black characters that Hollywood is selling today. Here is what Kenneth Robert Janken wrote in *White: The Biography of Walter White, Mr. NAACP* (The New Press, 2003):

> If the [NAACP] secretary had charmed producers, directors, and white stars, many of Hollywood's African American actors were downright hostile to his presence. They were furious that he came to town and

tried to change the movies without consulting them. The Mammy stereotype and clownish roles had provided a steady income for Hattie McDaniel, Butterfly McQueen, Stepin Fetchit, Clarence Muse, and a handful of others. Fearing the secretary's attempt to clean up the industry would result in their loss of livelihoods, they were gleeful when his first foray produced pious sentiment and little else. White disagreed, believing that his agitation would lead to expanded acting opportunities. But more to the point, he scorned his critics. Realistically, he said, he didn't expect thanks for his work, but he did expect those actors, who ultimately benefit from his negotiations "without their having to lift a finger," would remain gratefully silent.

Though White didn't accomplish much his agitation did succeed in getting David O. Selznick to replace the black rapist in Margaret Mitchell's *Gone with the Wind*, with a white one but now the black rapist is back in full force with *Precious,* and its business model *The Color Purple*; even President Obama was shown on MAD TV as a Mandingo stud in bed with Hillary Clinton. Sapphire says that we need more films about black rapists.

In the days of Walter White and Thurgood Marshall, the NAACP had some fight, but now this proud organization has been reduced to becoming a ward of corporate America. Promoting the artery clogging products of fast foods merchants. Taking money from criminal banks like the Bank of America and from FedEx, which recently had to pay 50 million dollars to black employees for racial discrimination, which is something that Annie Day of the Revolutionary Communist Party might note. She wrote a piece denouncing my *CounterPunch* article "The Selling Of Precious." She called me—you guessed it—a "misogynist," your typical white middle class feminist. Applying a double standard to white and black men; deferential toward their fathers, brothers, employers and gurus; unwilling to give the brothers some slack. This woman is part of a cult that revolves around a white patriarch—a cult that was abandoned by some blacks who accused it of "white chauvinism." A woman or her co-writer Carl Dix, a black man, will never lead this group. Their praise of the movie *Precious* jibes with that of Barbara Bush. Strange bedfellows indeed. Imagine the Revolutionary Communist Party having to wake up every morning next to Barbara Bush.

The awards were also sponsored by Disney whose *Princess and the Frog* demeans African religion, a fact noticed by the religion editor of the *Times*, Samuel G. Freedman (*New York Times*, 20 February 2010). And now the NAACP has given the segregated[2] Motion Picture Academy an excuse to perpetrate a cruel joke on black Americans on Sunday night by awarding an actress an Oscar whose role in the movie was to ask her daughter to assist her in achieving an orgasm. NAACP founders W.E.B. DuBois and Ida B. Wells, who risked her life to spark a drive to end the lynching of black men in the South, must be rolling over in their graves.

---

2. The Directors Guild of America reports that just 4 percent of its director membership is black; the Writers Guild of America says that 4.5 percent of members employed as TV writers and 3.2 percent of members employed as film writers are black (as of 2007, the last year for which data was available). And Paris Barclay, director-showrunner of *In Treatment* and co-chair of the DGA's Diversity Task Force, estimates that up to 82 percent of all episodes in television are "directed by Caucasian men."

The Wire Goes to College[1]

David Simon's *Homicide*, *The Corner*, and *The Wire* depend upon the image of the inner city as the center for the consumption and distribution of drugs. Though his supporters, black and white, deny this, the advertising for DVD's of his miniseries called *The Corner* reads "On the Front Lines of America's Drug War, One Family is Living in the Crossfire," while others might consider the borders and ports as the frontlines of the drug war since that's where tons of drugs are moved into the United States, daily.

My play *Hubba City* offers a more complicated view of the War on Drugs. It implicates gun storeowners, the banks who launder money, the real estate interests, and members of other ethnic groups. I was also acquainted with statistics that tended to portray inner city retail drug operations as a minor part of the drug war, with most of the drug consumption and sales happening elsewhere. Once in a while you'll read a story about heroin epidemics in the suburbs of Philadelphia,[2] overdoses occurring in Dallas suburbs from cheese heroin[3] or thousands of meth addicts in white rural areas[4] yet there is no white version of *The Wire*, even though most crack users are white. But to create a series about white meth and crack use wouldn't attract the fossil-fueled network advertisers, who feel that such a

---

1. An Edited Version of this essay appeared in *Playboy*, May 2010.
2. "Heroin Deaths Rise in Philadelphia Suburbs," *The New York Times*, March 20, 1995.
3. "'Cheese' flowing into area suburbs," *Dallas News*, Sept. 30, 2007.
4. "Crying Wolf About Meth Abuse?" *The New York Times*, August 11, 2005.

series would offend the media's target consumers, white men. The
same whites who are attracted to hip-hop music are attracted to *The
Wire* and so much money is being made from the invasion of the
inner city by sociologists, anthropologists, documentary producers
and Hollywood and television crews that I have proposed that the
inhabitants follow the practice that I have observed on Native
American reservations. Set up food and souvenir stalls.

When David Simon, *The Wire*'s producer, appeared on a 1997
Pacifica Network show, I called in and reminded him that the drug
issue was more complicated than *The Corner*, an earlier version of
The Wire, depicted it.

To lend authenticity to his product, Simon was accompanied by
a young black ghetto resident. Later, Simon went on Amy Goodman's
Show *Democracy Now* and had some laughs at the expense of the
youngster's lifestyle.

I had forgotten about my exchange with Simon until a few months
later, a *Times* writer called and said that Simon was charging that I
was against his writing about blacks because he was a "white man."
I told her that this wasn't the case. My objection to *The Wire* was
that dumping all of the country's pathologies upon the inner cities
as entertainment is a cliché. A number of movies, television shows,
news reports and town halls create the false impression that the
typical environment for drug activity is the inner city.

During a 2004 panel discussion held at Aix-en-Provence, I confronted one of the *The Wire* writers, Richard Price, who knows that
drug usage isn't black, exclusively. He's a recovering cocaine addict.
I was one of the earliest promoters of Price's work, but along the
way he began writing scripts for Hollywood based upon what he
called "brief forays into the ghetto." He has made so much money
by putting "Amos and Andy lines into the mouths of black characters," as even one of his supporters put it, that he has moved to
Harlem, and has been chosen by *The New York Times* to lead tours
of what once was the capital of Black America, over black historians, writers and old timers and story tellers who've lived there for
decades.

Virginia Heffernan of the *Times* would disagree with this writer's assessment. In her review of *The Wire*[5] she promised that the season would "knock the breath out of you." The storyline under review was about black teenage drug peddlers and her article was accompanied by the photo of four black teenage actors who were portrayed as drug dealers. Is there such a thing as a white teenage drug dealer? Sure is. White teenagers are 34 percent more likely to sell drugs than black teenagers[6] and while cocaine use among black teenagers is on the decline, that among white teenagers is on the upswing.[7] Two of the recent candidates for New York district attorney nearly boasted about their past cocaine use.[8] Do you suppose they bought their drugs from inner city black high school students? In the 2006 episode, praised by Ms. Heffernan and other critics, black youth were shown selling drugs, shoplifting, shooting crap, and murdering each other. This action was interrupted by scenes showing professional blacks so that the marketing aim of this grungy product wouldn't seem so obvious. Here as elsewhere Simon exploits young black people, shown in this episode speaking foul language and engaging in a fight with a rival gang using *bottles containing urine as their weapons!*

The hero of this piece is a white policeman turned teacher. When those who are hiring him for the job hear of his former profession, they treat his application with enthusiasm.

---

5. "High Learning in the Drug Trade for Four Baltimore Students," *The New York Times*, Sept. 9, 2008.

6. Journalist Tim Wise writes in the March 2001 on-line magazine *AlterNet.org*, "White high-school students are seven times more likely than blacks to have used cocaine; eight times more likely to have smoked crack; ten times more likely to have used LSD; and seven times more likely to have used heroin." There are more white high-school students who have used crystal methamphetamine (the most addictive drug on the street), than there are black students who smoke cigarettes. White youth ages twelve to seventeen are 34 percent more likely to sell drugs than their black counterparts. White youth are twice as likely to binge drink, and nearly twice as likely as blacks to drive drunk."

7. "Cocaine and White Teens." *The New York Times*, Jan. 9, 2009.

8. "Manhattan DA Dems Debate, Cocaine Use Admitted!" *Gothamist*, Jan. 28, 2009.

Ms. Heffernan, as though she were writing about a safari, described the teenagers as "would-be predators who might turn into prey." Ms. Heffernan described the "white negroes," who wrote the scripts as "lords of urban crime writing." I asked her had she read black crime writers, Iceberg Slim, Chester Himes, Donald Goines and Paula Woods. Ms. Heffernan in her reply pointed out that I only mentioned one woman writer and that she was more interested in the divide between men and women than blacks and whites, the kind of line from white feminists that has made black and brown women furious for over one hundred years, for where do they fall in Ms. Heffernan's divides? Are they black or women, and if Ms. Heffernan accepts them as women, do they have the same privileges as white women? According to the *Times*, white women in California do more drugs[9] than blacks and Latino men and women, but the jails are full of black and Latino women not white women. They do crack too, but don't get sentenced for it. Ms. Heffernan should talk to David Carr, her colleague at the *Times*. In his memoir[10] he includes scenes of white women passing the crack pipe around. Harvard and Yale women at the *Times* have a difficult time distinguishing the fake from the real when it comes to urban fiction. Michiko Kakutani raved over a ghetto urban memoir full of predators and the preyed upon written by a white woman named Margaret Seltzer. It was a fraud[11] and the publisher had to withdraw the book, leaving the editor, Sarah McGrath, and the publisher, Putnam, embarrassed.

I hadn't thought about *The Wire* again until I read an interview of David Simon's printed at *Jewish Weekly*[12]. He recalled my call into KPFA where he was being interviewed by Kris Welch. He said that I was "furious" and had accused the teenager of being manipulated

9. Mike Males, "This Is Your Brain on Drugs, Dad," *The New York Times*, Jan.3, 2007.

10. *The Night of the Gun: A reporter investigates the darkest story of his life. His own* by David Carr.

11. Clark Hoyt, "Fooled Again," *The New York Times*, March 16, 2008.

12. 'Wire' creator finds a muse on the streets of Baltimore," *Jweekly.com*, Jan. 18, 2010.

and led around by this white writer who was using him to foster a negative image of African Americans. My questions were aimed at Simon not the youngster but clearly my call was on his mind.

I told *JWeekly.com* that I wasn't opposed to white men writing about the ghetto. Over the years I've published scores of white men and women. I advised HBO to do something new. Maybe the family life of a suburban gun dealer who is sending illegal weapons into neighborhoods like mine.

If Ms. Heffernan and Ms. Kakutani's awkward wadings into the heart of darkness weren't enough, college professors of the kind who spend their lives on campuses and when traveling it's to visit another campus, have decided that they want to get down. Lord help us!

College courses about *The Wire* are spreading across the country and white students, students who can't identify John the Baptist or the Emperor Constantine, or identify who fought in World War II, are forming long lines to sign up for a course about a TV crime show that shows blacks as the sludge of humanity.

Polled about their knowledge of "American history, political thought, market economy and international relations" Harvard seniors scored D+[13]. What is one professor's answer to the crisis at Harvard? One of those teaching *The Wire* is Prof. Julius Wilson, who must be one cloistered individual to assert that David Simon's depiction of urban life provided a better understanding of that culture than anything written by a sociologist. I compared his inviting Simon to Harvard to a professor from Native American Studies inviting a producer of a John Wayne western to lecture about Wayne's westerns because they provided a great "understanding" of Native American life.

Wilson promised to send me a "thoughtful reply." It hasn't arrived. Not to be undone, Linda Williams at the University of California, an institution facing devastating budget cuts, is teaching *The Wire*. A woman prone to stunts, according to Professor Cecil

---

13. "Study shows US College students have inadequate knowledge of American history and institutions." Associated Press, Sept, 18, 2007.

Brown, Ms. Williams once built a lecture around Melvin Van Peebles' penis.

When I was a kid, my mother tried to explain to a seventh grade teacher why I was neglecting my homework. She blamed it on my staying up late and watching crime shows. Clearly, I was ahead of my time.

Diminutive Playwright Tackles Criminal Justice Dragon[1]

Professor Mel Watkins, a former staff member of *The New York Times Book Review*, in a farewell column for the *Times*,[2] warned that publishers would end up losing money by publishing women who saw profit in catering to the often bizarre fantasies that millions of whites hold about black men. He wrote, "It may be, as some black writers have suggested, that Ralph Ellison's insights into the white philanthropist portrayed in *Invisible Man* are more informative than one might have guessed, and that the enthrallment of whites with tales of depravity and violence in the black community is more than just a fictional theme."

Henry Louis Gates, Jr. was asked to respond to Watkins by feminist editor Rebecca Penny Sinkler. In his article, "Reclaiming Their Tradition,"[3] an article that has been removed from *The Times'* archives, he lauds black women writers and dismisses black male writers as a group, and since Gates had become the go-to intellectual for those who wish a CliffsNotes view of the black community, his comment had dire consequences for black male writers and diminished their access to the book buying public.

---

1. A version of this essay appeared in *Modern Drama*, University of Toronto, 2012.

2. "Sexism, Racism and Black Women Writers," Mel Watkins, *The New York Times*, June 15, 1986.

3. "Reclaiming Their Tradition," Henry Louis Gates, Jr. *The New York Times*, October 4, 1987.

In *The New York Times*,[4] novelist Diane Johnson seems to agree with Watkins. She describes a "largely white audience" as one that "press their noses against the window to see the black mama suckling her school age son, the black papa committing incest... perhaps what is exciting about the violence and depravity is that they confirm white fears." Since that time, Hollywood, television, newspapers, publishers and theaters have made hundreds of millions of dollars by thrilling those white fears, and the case of a man, who became the symbol of those white fears, O.J. Simpson, was used to earn billions.

Further evidence of the power of this "largely white audience" to determine which of those cultural and intellectual products from blacks are profitable is the current controversy that pits some prominent black women writers against Kathryn Stockett, author of *The Help*. Writing in *The Washington Post*,[5] Bernice L. McFadden complained about her lack of access to a white audience, now that Kathryn Stockett has debuted with her novel which features black women characters (her former maid is suing on the grounds that one of the characters is based upon her). McFadden asserts:

> Kathryn Stockett's novel *The Help*, published by a Penguin Books imprint, sold one million books within a year of publication. Her novel has gained accolades and awards, including the prestigious South African Boeke Prize. *The Help* was adapted for the screen; at the helm of production is the Academy Award-winning director and producer Steven Spielberg. Kathryn Stockett and Sue Monk Kidd are living the dream of thousands of authors, myself included. But they are not the first white women to pen stories of the black American South and be lauded for their efforts.

In a review of *The Help*, by C. Leigh McInnis,[6] he chastises Stockett for exploiting the evil black boogeyman theme. He writes:

---

4. "The Song of Toni Morrison," *The New York Times*, May 20, 1979.
5. "Black words, white publishers," Bernice L. McFadden, *The Washington Post*, Saturday, June 26, 2010.
6. Who or What Does *The Help* Help?: A Brief Review by C. Leigh McInnis. http://www.redochrelit.com/cmcinnis.html

And when Leroy [a character in the book] discovers that he has been fired from his job because of Minny contributing stories to the book, of course, all black savage Negro hell breaks out: "Minny panting and heaving. He throw the kids in the yard and lock me in the bathroom and say he gone light the house on fire with me locked inside!" (437). Thus, escaping life with Leroy, who by now has become the face of all African men, is as important as escaping white supremacy: "Still, what's important is, Minny's away from Leroy" (439). Whether Stockett knows it or not, this representation of African domestic violence is just one more use of writing as skin privilege, one more use of writing as a smokescreen to keep hidden the obscene abusive relationships that do exist in "white" marriages and partnerships. Stockett writes well, but she runs the risk of hopelessly reinforcing ideas of white supremacy, even if she does so unconsciously. Additionally, those who have profited from reading *Dessa Rose*, *Beloved*, and *The Autobiography of Miss Jane Pittman*—works that deal with recording someone else's story—may find that Stockett has consciously or unconsciously used the African male body as a symbol or smokescreen for all evil or merely to placate the supremacy of her white readers.

He agrees with me that black male "evil" is highly marketable. He writes: "the Negro boogeyman still sells as well as sex does." Leroy has even fewer lines than the black brute in *Precious*. We hear him threatening his wife, a maid, on the phone. She works for a woman who is an inept cook and housekeeper. Like most of the other white women in the film, she is a caricature. A dizzy blonde. While the black women are noble, dignified and suffering, the white women are like those in *White Chicks*, a 2004 American buddy film directed by Keenen Ivory Wayans and written and produced by Keenen Wayans, Shawn Wayans and Marlon Wayans. While Leroy is the movie's monster, the dizzy blonde's husband is in on the secret that she has hired a maid and the climax of the film occurs when the blonde shows that she indeed has learned how to fry chicken. This character helps the maid with her groceries. The villain of the film is a mean white girl, a racist, who gets her durthers, eventually. The rest of the country club white men in the film are benign. They are part of the upper crust, who don't belong to the Klan or The

White Citizens Council. The brutal action against one of the maids is carried out by the white underclass, the police. The race of Medgar Evers's murderer is not revealed. Not only do the black maids clean house and cook, but they're required to render unpaid talk therapy to these white women who are shown by the director and script writer as shallow and foolish. Though Kathryn Stockett's film does a service by providing testimonies from black maids about their exploitation, Katheryn Stockett is the real mean girl because she has earned millions from her black boogeyman book, while her inform-ants and co-writer received only a piddling amount.

The movie was directed and script written by a white male, Tate Taylor. What I can't understand is why black and white feminists who write black boogeyman books can't find women script writers and directors and producers to carry their projects to the screen.

The movie, though praised by white movie reviewers, women and men, caused outrage from black women critics, members of The Association of Black Women Historians whose members are Ida E. Jones, national director of ABWH and assistant curator at Howard University; Diana Ramey Berry, Tiffany M. Gill, and Kali Nicole Gross, lifetime members of the Association of Black Women Historians (ABWH) and associate professors at the University of Texas at Austin; and Janice Sumler-Edmond, lifetime member of ABWH and a professor at Huston-Tillotson University. Included in their statement was the following:

> ... the film is woefully silent on the rich and vibrant history of black civil rights activists in Mississippi. Granted, the assassination of Medgar Evers, the first Mississippi based field secretary of the NAACP, gets some attention. However, Evers' assassination sends Jackson's black community frantically scurrying into the streets in utter chaos and disorganized confusion—a far cry from the courage demonstrated by the black men and women who continued his fight. Portraying the most dangerous racists in 1960s Mississippi as a group of attractive, well dressed, society women, while ignoring the reign of terror perpetuated by the Ku Klux Klan and the White Citizens Council, limits racial injustice to individual acts of meanness.

We respect the stellar performances of the African American actresses in this film. Indeed, this statement is in no way a criticism of their talent. It is, however, an attempt to provide context for this popular rendition of black life in the Jim Crow South. In the end, *The Help* is not a story about the millions of hardworking and dignified black women who labored in white homes to support their families and communities. Rather, it is the coming-of-age story of a white protagonist, who uses myths about the lives of black women to make sense of her own. The Association of Black Women Historians finds it unacceptable for either this book or this film to strip black women's lives of historical accuracy for the sake of entertainment.

And so what is the result of the three decades of critical coddling by African American male critics, womanist critics, white feminist critics and delighted white male critics' nurturing a literature that focuses upon, in the words of Henry Louis Gates, Jr., "black male sexism?" A literature of the hot fudge sundae? A delicious literature? One that places the racism that African Americans continue to face in the background? Writing in *Poets & Writers*,[7] Tayari Jones is quoted:

> When people talk about black writers, or literary writers, or black literary writers, they tend to talk about social responsibility; they make reading and writing sound like a chore, as though the writing isn't supposed to be fun. But I was at this restaurant once, and there was this young woman, twenty something, reading a Twilight novel with this huge hot fudge sundae in front of her. You could tell she was just having a delicious time. That's what I want for my writing.

Jones says this as she pulls a sage-green afghan, a gift from a reader, over her lap. "I want it to be delicious." Delicious? Delicious? Is this the culmination of what was heralded as the Renaissance of black women's literature in *The New York Times* and *The Village Voice* in the late 1980s? A literature that as Ms. Jones writes puts race and politics in the background? A delicious literature.

---

7. "She is Ready: A Profile of Tayari Jones," by Rochelle Spencer, *Poets and Writers*, 4/07/2011.

By contrast many will find Ms. Kennedy's work hard to digest. Her powerful play, *Sleep Deprivation Chamber*, is about the rite of passage that most black men have to undergo whether they are underclass or overclass, because to the police, who often act as an instrument of white power, both groups are the same. Whether one is a black male living in the ghetto, a Harvard professor or most recently New York City's schools chancellor, Dennis M. Walcott, who was harassed by two plainclothes police officers during a traffic stop in Queens,[8] you are the target of what criminologist Jerome Miller calls a "search and destroy mission."[9]

Despite the abundance of evidence that blacks and Hispanics are singled out by law enforcement, to make such a claim is viewed as disrupting the post-race euphoria. Moreover, given the state of American prisons, which one writer described as gulags, where torture, medical malpractice and rape are used as methods of punishment, blacks and Hispanics are reluctant to send people to prison. Not to say that some blacks, whites, browns and reds don't need to be separated from the general population, but given the racist nature of drug law enforcement, two thirds of black inmates wouldn't be behind bars if they were white.[10] According to the *Times*, the typical substance abuser in California is a white woman[11] yet California jails are full of black and Hispanic women who are there for violation of the drug laws.

With the introduction of "black boogeyman literature," instead of a white supremacist society, the traditional target of black literature, the target became the oppressed themselves.

---

8. "Police Look Into Complaint by Walcott After Traffic Stop," Al Baker, *The New York Times*, April 20, 2011.

9. Search and Destroy: African-American Males in the Criminal Justice System by Jerome G. Miller (November 22, 2010).

10. "Race vs Justice," *USA Today*, April 27, 2000.

11. "This Is Your Brain On Drugs," Mike Males, January 3, 2007: "Few experts would have suspected that the biggest contributors to California's drug abuse, death and injury toll are educated, middle-aged women living in the Central Valley and rural areas, while the fastest-declining, lowest-risk populations are urban black and Latino teenagers. Yet the index found exactly that. These are the sorts of trends we need to understand if we are to design effective policies."

To broach subjects like the use of blacks in Africa and in the United States for pharmaceutical experiments,[12] as I did in my play, *Body Parts*, or America's racist and corrupt criminal justice system, Adrienne Kennedy's subject, is seen as being involved in "old fights" or to be "angry" or "paranoid." When I wrote about my negative experiences with the police, I was challenged by John McWhorter, writing in *Commentary*,[13] a magazine where Charles Murray's ideas about black intellectual inferiority have found a home. McWhorter is a fellow at the Manhattan Institute, which inspired Mayor Giuliani's policies that included the ethnic removal of Manhattan's blacks, and the notorious stop and frisk measures during which thousands of black and Hispanic men were stopped by the police without cause which was not only unconstitutional but a case of the kind of time theft which victimizes blacks in every day life. Charles Blow, a columnist for *The New York Times*, cites police harassment as a factor that contributed to the exodus from New York City by thousands of African Americans.[14]

Time theft happened to me after I was arrested by a policeman in New York whom I accused of taking a bribe, and it occurs in *Sleep Deprivation Chamber* because both Teddy, the son, and Suzanne Alexander, his mother, lost time as a result of having to meet with lawyers and make court appearances. Alexander spends time writing letters to politicians much to the chagrin not only of her attorney but the prosecutor. "I can tell Edelstein thinks I may jeopardize Teddy's case by writing too many letters. He told me to write two: one to the governor and one to the county manager. I have written seventeen, but I haven't told him."

But as an artist she is able to make up for this lost time by including the letters in *Sleep Deprivation Chamber*.

---

12. Nigerians Receive First Payments for Children Who Died in 1996 Meningitis Drug Trial, By Donald G. McNeill, Jr. *The New York Times*, August 11, 2011.

13. From *Commentary Magazine*, "Still losing The Race," by John H. McWhorter, February 2004.

14. "Escape From New York - NYTimes.com" by Charles Blow, *The New York Times*, March 18, 2011.

Time theft happens to blacks each day because they are subjected to extra scrutiny in their trade negotiations. Buying clothes in a department store. Cashing a check in a bank or in my case, doing months of paperwork for a mortgage only to be turned down even though my credit rating is excellent. As long as blacks lose hundreds of millions of dollars per year as a result of racial profiling, those who argue for a post-race America are either naïve or collaborators with a system that oppresses.

By tackling an issue, that of police brutality, Ms. Kennedy risked the alienation of the white audiences at which American producers aim their theater. From blacks, contemporary white audiences, the people who can afford the orchestra seats, want something "delicious." Something guilt free. Something that places race in the background. Something that places the responsibility of the entire world's evil on the shoulders of black men.

Given the current climate where the men who give out Pulitzers prefer the kind of portrait of blacks painted by the Manhattan Institute and those presented in their newspapers, newspapers that always side with the police and the prosecution, I can imagine a New York bourgeois audience recoiling at Kennedy's line, "His lawyer said the judge (in Virginia) always sided with the police, and the police would be sure to have secret witnesses as a surprise."

Adrienne Kennedy was not out for money or prizes when she co-wrote *Sleep Deprivation Chamber* with her son Adam Kennedy. She was not out to play favor with middle-class white audiences who would find Professor Robert Hampshire of *Ohio State Murders* a bummer. Certainly, Michael Criscuolo[15] found this white male killer a turn off.

Sleep Deprivation Chamber might be the most devastating indictment of the country's criminal justice system yet staged. And since the play is based upon the police beating of her son, Adam, Ms. Kennedy, the playwright, shows remarkable restraint as she uses her

---

15. *New York Theater Review,* Michael Criscuolo, November 4, 2007 writing in *nytheatre.com* review November 4, 2007.

sense of irony, her great gift, in a calm presentation of the facts. American blacks are familiar with the scenes in this play. If they haven't been the victims of police brutality, they know someone who has, even though black and white progressives believe that middle class blacks whom they call house Negroes have more advantages than field Negroes. Ms. Kennedy during her research uncovers the extent of the problem from which no class of blacks is immune. She writes: "By now I had a list of cases where black men were beaten: athletes, college students. It was long."

I live in the ghetto where sometimes-fatal results occur from a simple encounter like a traffic stop. A defective brake light provides the police with an excuse to pry into one's business and maybe find some evidence that will send the black or Hispanic to be used as cheap labor by private prisons that are earning billions in profits.[16] In fact a study says that prison lobbyists are urging longer sentences to take advantage of this cheap labor, which recalls the convict lease system of the post Civil War era. During that period, the excuse for sending blacks to provide cheap labor for white businesses was the vagrancy law; in our own time it's the traffic violation.

I was stopped for not coming to a complete stop, a scam that the police run in ghetto neighborhoods. The fine is one hundred dollars. When I went to traffic court in Oakland, California, to pay the one hundred dollar fine, I discovered that over 90 percent of those present to pay fines were either black or Hispanic.

And so Suzanne Alexander's theatrical son Teddy's troubles begin with an incident involving a broken brake light and he is beaten in front of his home by a policeman. The policeman drags Teddy across the driveway while kicking him in the stomach and back and punching him repeatedly. He testifies during the trial that he attempted to be civil with the policeman. He says, "Officer what seems to be the problem? I live here, this is my house. Can I help you?" The Kennedys record the route that black men caught in a situation like

---

16. *Slavery by Another Name: The Re-Enslavement of Black Americans From the Civil War to World War II*, by Douglas A. Blackmon, January 13, 2009.

Teddy's must negotiate before either being sent to prison or acquitted. Their black female lawyer can't believe that he, a young black
man, has never been arrested. She urges him to plead guilty and
receive a suspended sentence, the kind of bargain that thousands of
the poor accept each day whether they are guilty or not. With this
lawyer, and a black policewoman, who draws a gun on Teddy's
father, David, who approached the scene of the beating to find out
what was happening, Kennedy departs from the chocolate fudge
sundae school of black womanist writers that requires saintly mar-
tyred black women to be surrounded by evil black men, the formula
for chic lit, hi and low, and in films like *The Color Purple* and *The
Help*. With these portraits the Kennedys enter Hannah Arendt country. She also offends the Walker/Gates/Smith directive that black
women characters must be positive,[17] a directive that dehumanizes
black women and one that their icon, Zora Neale Hurston, refused
to follow.

Ms. Kennedy's portraits of black men and women are also too
complex for the white men who control the Pulitzers, who are press-
ing their noses against the window with the rest of the voyeurs
searching for signs of black depravity. The black Pulitzer judges, who
have no power, tried to warn them that Janet Cooke's *Washington
Post* series about an eight-year-old black heroin addict was fake,[18]
but they gave her series a Pulitzer anyway only to be embarrassed.
With this history, it came as no surprise that one went to a novel
about a black slave master.[19] Since Janet Cooke's prize, the white male
Pulitzer jury has rewarded a succession of novels and plays that use
the black male as a piñata. This is another roadblock preventing Ms.
Kennedy from receiving a Pulitzer because David doesn't fit the
"black boogeyman" cast. He enters Suzanne Alexander's life at a
point where she has suffered unspeakable tragedies, the murder of

---

17. Claudia Tate, *Black Women Writers at Work*, Continuum, 1998.

18. The Pulitzer Hoax-Who Can Be Believed? By HP-Time.com; Thomas
Griffith, *Time Magazine*, Monday, May 04, 1981.

19. *The Known World* [Paperback], Edward P. Jones, HarperCollins, 2003.

her twins. He's finished law school. His father was a lawyer for the NAACP.

With her portrait of black men in *Ohio State Murders* and *Sleep Deprivation Chamber* as talented, intellectuals find her as being out of sync with the times. David travels with Franz Fanon in North Africa. She writes, "[Patrice] Lumumba was like my husband trying to find Genesis in the midst of golden savannas. He wanted the black man to rise." His mental problems begin with his being jailed in Algeria and his being disappointed with black progress. "His state in the last years had been despondency, and the medications he took for the injuries he suffered when he was imprisoned briefly in Algeria in 1961 robbed him of stamina." Of his teaching at Stanford David comments: "Even though they honor me," he often said, "this is like a white country club." He is given to memory loss. "David walked from his cottage by lake Lagunita (at Stanford) down Therese to Tresidder and past the Old Union, took the bus to the terminal to San Francisco and vanished."

The son is directing *Hamlet*. Throughout the play Kennedy insists upon showing black men who are devoted to uplifting the community. Good citizens. "I would hear my father and his friends discuss (as they always did) how to make Cleveland a better place for Negroes, how to raise money for the Quincy Library and for the cornerstone ceremony for the Central Y." Her black men are not uniformly positive. They are balanced. They can be brutes as well as professors and directors of *Hamlet*.

In her letters to officials including then Governor Wilder, who had his own hostile encounter with an airport screener who didn't recognize him as a former governor and grabbed him by the throat,[20] which refutes the stateside Marxist argument that members of the black middle class are treated differently from the black working class, she reminds him that her family is one of good breeding. "Why, why should we have to defend ourselves with character letters when

---

20. "Guard Fired After Grabbing Douglas Wilder By Throat," *Orlando Sentinel*, March 8, 1995.

we were innocent? All our lives our families had tried to fit in American society and improve our situation." This was the Governor Wilder who started a controversy when he said that white college students should be charged with drug violations in the same manner as inner city youth.[21]

Though shows like *The Wire*, which appeal to the same audience that Diane Johnson wrote about in 1979, might show crime as a problem of the black ghetto, and deserving of an aggressive police force, Kennedy points out that the men of Suzanne Alexander's family are aristocrats, not the incest perpetrator of *Precious*, a black-skinned beast with two or three lines. Teddy's father is the head of Africa/USA, yet when he seeks answers about the beating of Suzanne's son, the aforementioned black policewoman draws a gun on him. To Governor Wilder, Suzanne insists that: "All our lives we have tried to fit in American society and improve our society." She tells the governor of her son's achievements as a student leader. "He was the president of the African-American students group at Riverdale." She fears that the jury would be a jury that black defendants fear. White southerners of the kind who acquitted the men who killed Emmett Till.

She invokes Emmett Till, who, according to one of the killers whose testimony appears in an FBI report[22] was not killed for whistling at a white woman but for telling his attackers, "I'm just as good as you." Before he said that, the drunken men were going to leave

---

21. "When Cops Came to Campus," Joe Treen, *People Magazine*, July 1, 1991: "The raids brought mixed reaction on and off campus. The university administration, Virginia's Governor Douglas Wilder and the *Washington Post* all backed the busts. And blacks were delighted. 'The raid was past due,' says former Charlottesville NAACP president Drewary Brown. 'I hate to think of anybody's son or daughter getting arrested, but if it was my child downtown here, they'd have gotten him long ago.'"

22. March, 2007, the FBI released a summary of its 8000-page report of its investigation of the murder of Emmett Till. This report also includes the 354-page transcript of the 1955 murder trial of J. W. Milam and Roy Bryant. The transcript had been lost for decades, but in the course of their investigation, the FBI located a faded copy and re-transcribed it.

him off at a hospital. Alexander tells the governor, "Our son is being persecuted by the Arlington Police just as surely as it happened in the Deep South in the 1930s or during Emmett Till's time."

Alan Dershowitz got into trouble from some white people, whom the police are vowed to protect by keeping blacks out of their neighborhoods or monitoring blacks who drive expensive cars, or who date their daughters, for saying that the police are trained to lie and that there is even a term for it: testilying.[23] Under withering cross examination the officer, who arrested Teddy, admits that he didn't follow procedures and his testimony is full of inconsistencies including his inability to provide evidence for Teddy striking him. These inconsistencies are apparent to the judge who dismisses the case. Teddy was lucky. In the majority of cases involving blacks and Hispanics, those who can't hire lawyers, the district attorneys and judges, who have to work with the police, collude to send thousands of blacks and Hispanics to prison whether they are guilty or not.

Another reason that Ms. Kennedy will not win a Pulitzer Prize is because, just as blacks are the ones most likely to be confined in a physical prison, she is confined to an aesthetic prison by those who impose a few ways of telling a story upon black artists. Unorthodoxy is frowned upon. As Lorraine Hansberry remarked to Mike Wallace, Broadway producers have a problem with cerebral blacks.

Ms. Kennedy has been a risk taker since the beginning of her career. In her debut, Obie—award—winning play, *Funnyhouse of a Negro*, Ms. Kennedy showed her ability to crisscross time and mix and sample from popular and classical culture, using historical and political figures in novel ways. So it is with this play in which *Hamlet* by Shakespeare, *Ohio The Murders* by Suzanne Alexander, and the police incident and trial are intertwined. Intertwined is the word used by Adrienne Kennedy when writing about the techniques used to write *Funnyhouse*, which was assembled from a "raging mass of paragraphs." *Ohio State Murders* and *Dracula* are taking place.

---

23. Testimony of Alan M. Dershowitz, House of Representatives Judiciary Committee, December 1, 1998.

Rodney King's case is taking place. "We were all still upset over the Rodney King beating."

The writer remembers her childhood in Cleveland. David, the father, is suffering memory lapses. He traveled with the noted author Franz Fanon in North Africa and suffers depression over the slow progress that blacks are making in their quest for freedom. Kennedy is in Cleveland for a tribute, but the tribute becomes an embarrassment as she is treated shabbily by a local playwright, her host, and is insulted by the producer who wishes to incorporate descriptions of the playwright that her sister-in-law, Alice Alexander, had mentioned in an interview. She complains: "I'm beginning to regret this project. When you wrote me last year you said you wanted to do a brief piece on my Ohio State years. Now you're reaching in parts of all my life. It wasn't in our agreement." The local playwright picks up on Suzanne Alexander's disappointment. She says, "Sure, I sense your disdain for me." They want to use Alice to tamp down the force of the play, which is embarrassing to those who organized the festival that is supposed to be a tribute to her because it exposes the racist treatment that she received at the school. She is asked to discuss the violent imagery in her work, but instead of the violent imagery that arises from her dreams—the beheadings, etc.—she discusses the racist treatment that she received while attending Ohio State, which she entered in 1949.

The black girls are separated from white girls, some of whom are rude to them. Though the black women have sororities, they don't have "houses" like the white girls. She is spied upon by Miss Dawson who reads her diaries to the dorm committee that concludes that she is "unsuitable" for campus life and, after her baby is born, she is not allowed to return to campus life. Her parents are humiliated and she is sent to New York to live with a relative. Look at what Adrienne Kennedy's Suzanne Alexander has to endure during her Cleveland "tribute." Those who are paying tribute to her disrespect her. She has to relive the bad experience she had at the school that extended her the invitation, which includes a revisiting of the murders of her twins. (Whether this happens to Adrienne Kennedy or Suzanne

Alexander, who she calls herself, is unclear, she writes: "This winter after my sixtieth birthday I began to write about myself in the third person. I could not stop myself. It became... Suzanne said, Suzanne did.") A policeman has beaten her son and the local playwright who is supposed to host the festival is murdered.

Adrienne Kennedy is one of the few survivors of those who were mentioned as being at the forefront of the 1980s black women's Renaissance. The great Toni Cade Bambara is deceased. Shirley Anne Williams and Carlene Hatcher Polite, whom some credit with beginning modern black feminist fiction, are deceased. Gayl Jones has suffered incredible tragedies. A major innovator Ntozake Shange has endured devastating health setbacks.

I might have disagreements with a handful of a black women writers, the most prominent among them surrogates of powerful white feminists, who find it easier to join in an attack on the brothers than to show up to protest the end of social programs that affect millions of women, black, white, brown, yellow and red, but I would be among those to admit that you have to be strong to be a serious black woman writer who rejects the chocolate fudge sundae marketing strategy or the effigizing of black men.

The Suzanne Alexander character has appeared before in Adrienne Kennedy's *Alexander Plays,* a beautiful surrealist exercise that combines Freudian psychoanalysis; *The Dramatic Circle,* devoted to a reading of Bram Stoker's *Dracula* and a parade of landmarks and characters from English History. The Alexander of this play is in the midst of a psychological crisis as a result of the absence of her husband Dave Alexander. The contrast between the Suzanne of *The Dramatic Circle* and the Suzanne of *Sleep Deprivation Chamber* is striking. It is as though with the police beating of her son, reality threw cold water in the face of the somnambulist Suzanne of *The Dramatic Circle.*

Trouble Beside the Bay[1]

Jean Quan may be the first in many categories—the first Asian-American and first woman to be mayor of Oakland—but she is far from the city's first chief executive to face off with its police force. While dozens of mayors around the country have had to deal with Occupy movements, only Ms. Quan has seen the initially peaceful protests turn into street violence and even a general strike—a turn almost wholly attributable to the brutality of the city police.

In their zeal to fight back, however, the protesters, many of them white out-of-towners, have left locals unsure of who really has their best interests at heart.

On October 25 the world saw an Oakland police force that blacks have had to deal with for decades—even before the Black Panthers organized to protest the shooting of a black youth in the 1960s, a time when the police were said to be recruited from the South because they knew how to handle African Americans. In a video watched worldwide, an officer in riot gear fired a tear gas canister at a protester; the victim, an Iraq War veteran, later underwent surgery for his wounds. When some occupiers went to help him, another canister was lobbed at them.

That same night officers allegedly used rubber bullets during an assault on campers in Frank H. Ogawa Plaza. If so, that would violate the department's rules of engagement. Those rules were adopted in 2003, after the police assaulted antiwar protesters at the Port of

---

1. A version of this article appeared in *The New York Times* on November 8, 2011.

Oakland, even injuring some longshoremen who happened to be passing by.

The force's viciousness, particularly against blacks and Latinos, is legendary. In one recent case, a group of officers known as the Riders, who racked up an impressive list of drug takedowns, were accused of brutality, kidnapping and planting evidence on their road to arrests. Another officer, nicknamed "Audie Murphy," after the sharpshooting war hero and film star, shot four suspects and killed three. So little has been done to reform the force that a federal judge has threatened to take the entire department into receivership.

Many of Oakland's officers don't even live in the city, but rather its suburbs, a fact that helps maintain a strong "us versus them" worldview. (At a recent community meeting I proposed that the city study a plan, developed by Detroit, that rents foreclosed homes to police officers for as little as $1,000, to keep them in the city.)

The police still have influence in City Hall, though: their union repeatedly and vocally criticizes elected officials, including the mayor. For years it opposed making officers pay toward their pensions like other city workers. (The union agreed to start contributing in July.)

Mayor Quan initially supported the police after the October 25 clashes. Keith Olbermann called for her resignation; so did Michael Moore, who made a nuisance of himself by barging into Oakland Highland General Hospital, demanding to see the injured veteran (who had already been transferred to another hospital). Support for the protests grew, with statements of sympathy coming in from Cairo and Düsseldorf, Germany.

Such pressure may explain why Ms. Quan later apologized for the use of excessive force by the police, and is now trying to take a hands-off approach to the matter. Needless to say, the police department has been critical, saying it was "confused" by her latest moves.

All of this has left Oakland's blacks and Latinos in a difficult position. They rightly criticize the police, but they also criticize the other invading army, the whites from other cities, and even other states, whom they blame for the vandalism that tends to break out whenever there is a heated protest in town: from the riots after the murder of Oscar Grant by a transit police officer in 2009, to the violence of the last two weeks downtown and, most recently, near the port.

Someday we may discern the deeper historical meaning of these latest events. For now, what's striking are the racial optics. How did Asian Americans respond to the sight of a diminutive Asian-American mayor being hooted off the stage by a largely white crowd at an October 27 rally? And where was the sympathy when, in years past, unarmed blacks and Hispanics were beaten or killed? Why did it take the injury of a white protester to attract attention?

Meanwhile, those hurt most by the protests are local business owners and workers, many of them minorities. Jose Dueñas, the chief executive of the Hispanic Chamber of Commerce of Alameda County, blamed the Occupy movement for stalled economic activity. "We've got no events planned, people are pulling back," he told a local newspaper. "We don't blame them." The cash-strapped city has spent over $1 million so far in occupation-related costs.

Local activism has been pushed aside as well. Even as Occupy Oakland has occupied the Bay Area headlines, hundreds of black, white and Latino parents met to oppose plans to close five schools in black neighborhoods. The following day there was hardly a single line of newsprint about the meeting.

The Occupy movement has important things to say. But in its hurry to speak, it risks shutting out those who have been waiting their turn for a long time.

"She Wanted It"

Whether or not former IMF head Strauss-Kahn is guilty, his defense that the encounter between him and a black hotel worker was consensual is one that has been used, historically, by white men charged with sexual assault against black women. The attitude of some white men that black women, regardless of their class position, are always hot, ready and available to them, has been a factor in the history of the Civil Rights Movement. The harassment of New York black women, by the NYPD, America's Gestapo, is now under fire from Hispanic and black groups for its notorious "stop-and-frisk" policy, which subjects black and Hispanic men to the sometimes violent actions of the police without cause. In the 1900s both blacks and Jews were subjected to police violence, something about which Mayor Michael Bloomberg, who endorses the "stop-and-frisk" measures, must be ignorant.

Commentators who trace the beginning of an alliance between blacks and Jews to the modern period are in error. The alliance begins in the early 1900s over the issue of NYPD violence against both groups. Marilynn S. Johnson in her book *Street Justice* writes (p. 80): "The common abuse of Jews and African Americans at the hands of the police during these years thus laid the groundwork for the black-Jewish alliance that would become particularly important in the 1930s and 1940s."[1]

---

1. Marilynn S. Johnson, *Street Justice: A History of Police Violence in New York City*, Beacon Press, 2004.

The assumption that a black woman alone on the street was there for solicitation led to The Tenderloin Riot of 1900, in which ten thousand people participated.

On August 12, 1900 a black man, Arthur Harris, intervened to defend the honor of his girlfriend, Mary Eno, who was in the process of being arrested by plainclothes officer Robert Thorpe. Thorpe was killed. Johnson notes that the charge of solicitation was used, regularly, against black women. Still is.

Dori Maynard, head of the Maynard Institute, which has trained hundreds of minority journalists and was named for her father, the late publisher of the Oakland Tribune, was recently escorted from a Hampton Inn for talking to a white man. I asked her whether she'd received an apology. She answered, "I never did receive a formal apology from any of the entities involved. And when I asked for a sit down, they only agreed if I signed away my rights to talk about the original insult. Obviously, I couldn't agree to that."

Though Rosa Park's refusing to yield her seat to a white person is seen as a spontaneous act, Parks was an activist long before this historical moment. She was one of those who assisted in the 1944 case of Recy Taylor who was gang raped by white men as she was walking home from church. They threatened her with shotguns. Their defense was that she was a prostitute and they paid her.

Two all white male juries refused to indict the rapists. The rape and the nation-wide controversy that accompanied it is viewed as one of the events that led to the formation of the modern Civil Rights Movement.[2]

Carole Simpson in her book, *NewsLady*, reports that she was the target of sexual aggression from her white male colleagues whose ideas about black women are also based upon superstition and myth.

These are not Southern good old boys carousing about looking for a good time at the expense of a black victim, but men who work at networks that have been accused of having a liberal slant.

---

2. Danielle L. McGuire, *At The Dark End Of The Street, Black Women, Rape, and Resistance: A New History of the Civil Rights Movement from Rosa Parks to the Rise of Black Power*, Knopf, 2010.

Though some New York newspapers have blasted Strauss-Kahn with some colorful entertaining and combustible prose, other copy contains the wink and nod of admiration for his sexual prowess.

While nobody seems to care about the tastes of the average rape suspect's family, his family is shown as civilized people who own Piccasos.

While black and Hispanic defendants are pictured with mug shots of sullen faces, a San Francisco newspaper printed a photo of Strauss-Kahn with a broad grin. Photos in U.S.A. *Today* and MSNBC had him smiling. The cat that swallowed the canary.

The good old boys who run the media seem to be saying "way to go Dominique," as a salute to his being a satyr.

PART III

As Relayed By Themselves

An Interview with Lou Gossett, Jr.[1]

I interviewed Lou Gossett, Jr. in his lovely Malibu home on June 25, 2010. His talk ranged over a number of topics. Despite his distinguished career as a stage and screen actor and Oscar winner, the segregationists who run Hollywood will not cast him in the roles that meet his high standards.

Since he talks back and is picky, he gets called "difficult."

The Hollywood that is "liberal" to the right and that fund raises for a black president, still adheres to Jim Crow practices. Black actors do not get paid as much as white ones. A good old boys' club is a barrier against diversity. Black membership of the Screen Writers Guild is almost nonexistent. The Board of Governors that picks Oscar winners is all white! Black, Hispanic and Asian American women get roles as prostitutes. Check out *Brooklyn's Finest*, where, like in *American Gangster* the screen is littered with black corpses, and like David Simon's neo-Nazi *The Wire,* blacks are scapegoated as the chief distributors and consumers of drugs, and, using a tip from the *Captivity Narratives* of the 1700s, Richard Gere rescues white women from their evil black captors (in the 1700s it was evil Indian captors).

Black men play pimps and criminals, when they have failed at both professions, though once in a while you get someone who is as

---

1. A version of this interview appeared at Counterpunch.org, September 24-26, 2010.

clever as Howard Smith, who staged the costliest embezzlement in Wells Fargo history, the kind of crime for which white men get light sentences and get to go to Club Feds' tennis courts. And dine on Long Island duck.

Lou Gossett, Jr.'s memoir, *An Actor and a Gentleman*, was published in 2010 by Wiley. He was a great host. He was very friendly as my entourage and I took over his house. His assistant was friendly and so were his dogs. Our driver, Joyce Sumbi, with whom we spent most of the afternoon, entertained us with stories about her family, her life in Los Angeles. She was a retired librarian. She talked about meeting Walter Mosley and Terry McMillan at a book fair. She died about a month later.

ISHMAEL REED: *Was your father Italian?*

LOU GOSSETT: He was adopted by an Italian family. The reason why is if you go to Coney Island there are huge newsstands located near the subways. They have an Italian connection. They owned those. A man who worked for them owned one of the largest ones in America. He adopted my father.

ISHMAEL REED: *How did that come about?*

LOU GOSSETT: That came about because when my grandfather and my grandmother got divorced, they abandoned my two uncles and my aunt. And in order to save them from going to boarding school or wherever they sent them, orphanage, my father got a job and sent two of them to the military school and one to nursing school. They were all going to go, he was going to send all of them, and they needed someone to adopt those remaining. The Italian mother said to my father, "I'll adopt you." My father was adopted. He grew up in the Italian household.

ISHMAEL REED: *What part of Italy did they come from?*

LOU GOSSETT: Sicily. They were the Sylvester family. My father's best friend, Georgie Terra, was an Italian guy. The children and the cousins and nieces and nephews were children of the Mafia. Those were the children he grew up with. If you want to go to a safe neighborhood, go to where the Mafia is.

ISHMAEL REED: *Your father was in politics.*

LOU GOSSETT: He divorced my mother first and then he got a brand new car every year. He earned a nice piece of change. I didn't know that at the time, but he was very popular. He had a nice piece of change. This was after the Depression.

ISHMAEL REED: *At the Actors Studio was Marilyn Monroe very serious?*

LOU GOSSETT: She was very serious. She called me on the phone asking me to act with her. I blew it by my stammering. Someone else got the part.

ISHMAEL REED: *The Actors Studio. James Dean?*

LOU GOSSETT: We used to hang out together. There were four of us who used to hang out together. James Dean played the lead in Andre Gide's *The Immoralist*, with Geraldine Page. I was appearing in *Take a Giant Step*. I was sixteen in 1953. The lead was Jane White, the daughter of Walter White (former head of the NAACP). James Dean, Ben Carruthers, myself, and a couple of others used to hang out together. We'd sustain ourselves with Horn & Hardart jelly doughnuts and Italian sandwiches.

ISHMAEL REED: *You got on television.*

LOU GOSSETT: I did. Right after that.

Ishmael Reed: *You did a line about Jesus Christ that caused controversy. It was, "Jesus Christ, the sergeant is coming."*

LOU GOSSETT: Let me tell you about that. My great grandmother came to see the show. There was a woman who played my grandmother. There was a line where I said, "Damn it, Grandma, I'm not going to do that." After the show was over my grandmother slapped me upside the face. POW! I said, "What did you slap me for? That was a line in the play." "You can't curse like that." She couldn't understand that it wasn't real and that it was just a line in the play. That was what that was for.

ISHMAEL REED: *In your book you praised Lew Wasserman.*

LOU GOSSETT: He came from Detroit. He was one of those society people who were formerly poor but started making new money. Remember those "Movies of the Week" at Universal Studios? That's where he came from. He started Universal's Movies of the Week. Some of the actors in the first movie were Patrick O'Neal, William Redfield, Melvyn Douglas, Anne Baxter, and Don Winter, and Gig Young –all of those people. I played the detective and I had to find out the killer. The script had a bunch of rich people in a psych ward with crazy stuff going on. One of the characters was played by Melvyn Douglas. I was told to push him out of the way. I thought, "No, I can't do that. That's Melvyn Douglas." Seeing my nervousness, he said, "Lay it on me!" That society was beautiful. The other society was the police and blue-collar workers in Los Angeles in 1968.

ISHMAEL REED: *We'll get to that. When I go to the movies now these special effects during the previews—they're disturbing. Noisy. Violent.*

LOU GOSSETT: The people you see with all the piercings and tattoos are the wizards who do those special effects. You see them in the lab doing the animation. They have long red, blue, green hair. There are so many of them, but they do brilliant things. *Avatar* was gorgeous. There are good stories in there, but when used in other movies they're similar to those violent video games. Characters using deadly weapons. The children follow these movies.

ISHMAEL REED: *You really can't tell the difference between a movie and a video game, nowadays. Do you think that special effects driven movies are eliminating character?*

LOU GOSSETT: Yes. That's not what I came here to do.

ISHMAEL REED: *Your father was a very fascinating man.*

LOU GOSSETT: He was. He never said, "I love you," but when he died there were several carefully prepared scrapbooks he'd left in the bedroom. He was my number one fan. My mother was outgoing, but my father was cold. He had a tough time. He had to work hard. His father was like Jack Johnson. He had gold teeth and was a play-boy. He had women taking care of him all of the time. He was a colorful man, full of life. He was overcompensating. He was the big man in the barbershop where I went to get a haircut.

ISHMAEL REED: *You got a picture of him with a lot of liquor bottles in front of him.*

LOU GOSSETT *(pointing to a photo in the book)*: That was my bed-room, which was also the living room. They would start out dancing doing the lindy hop and the boogie-woogie to Cab Calloway, Count Basie and Louis Jordan. Then they would start fighting with each other. They would fight all out in the street until they went home and fell asleep. That happens in Africa. But that's not the best of us.

ISHMAEL REED: *NYU and Greenwich Village.*

LOU GOSSETT: I was acting on Broadway and then I went to college. That's when I met you. My second theater role was in a play starring Shirley Booth, of *Comeback Little Sheba*. I had a small part. The mail boy. I made money though. I took a leave of absence from school and went to New Haven, Boston and Philadelphia with the cast. I earned money for school. I had three or four funny lines. Our last stop was Wilmington, Delaware. There was a nice hotel room. The room service took a long time to get to me, though. This was Wilmington. I had to be careful. I walked the streets and found the New England Grill. I must have been eighteen. People said, "Hello." I waited for an hour for my food. They told me, finally, "We don't serve colored people here." POW! I did poorly in rehearsal and was in danger of being let go and having to return to New York. Shirley Booth said, "Wait a minute, he's been doing well." I told Shirley Booth what had happened at the New England Café and started to cry. She told me that she would handle it and to go to the hotel and relax. The next morning a maid with food and invitations to all the restaurants and private homes awakened me. Shirley Booth had contacted the DuPonts who were throwing a party in her honor. She told them that she would not attend the party unless I was invited and, "If you don't treat this young man properly, we are packing up and moving to New Haven, Connecticut. And I can assure you no future pre-Broadway shows will ever come to Wilmington again." The DuPonts were major contributors to the theatrical society, including Penny DuPont who was my age and who became friends with me. That was that society. They stood up for me. From childhood until Hollywood we were one. The society full of people like Marlon Brando.

ISHMAEL REED: *Did you know Bill Gunn?*

LOU GOSSETT: Oh, yes. Very well. What a great writer. My first movie was *The Landlord*. That was his work.

ISHMAEL REED: *We did a retrospective of* Personal Problems. *It was his last movie. It was produced by Steve Cannon and me.*

LOU GOSSETT: Never heard of it.

ISHMAEL REED: *When you arrived in Los Angeles, the studio put you up in the Beverly Hills Hotel and rented a fancy car. You had an encounter with the LAPD whose racist treatment of minorities continues to this day.*

LOU GOSSETT: I had trouble with them within my first twenty-four hours. When I came out to Los Angeles I flew in a propeller airplane and the stewardesses were so nice and they would slice the meat for you. A limo came to the plane. The William Morris Agency planned all this. I said, "Whose limo is this?" "This is for you." This was in the '60s now. They put my suitcase in the back seat and took me to the Beverly Hills Hotel. I was greeted with "Good evening, sir." They put me up in the presidential suite. They took good care of me. I rented a car. They gave me a white Ford Fairlane convertible with red leather interior from Hertz. I said "LOOK AT ME!" I jumped in and put on Sam Cooke. It took me four and a half hours to get to the Beverly Hills Hotel. It usually took twenty minutes. Every one hundred yards I heard, "Pull over. You fit the description of someone who stole a car like this." They were lined up Sunset, all the way down. It took me four and half hours to go from Crescent Heights to Sunset Boulevard to the Beverly Hills Hotel. I was eating good food at the hotel. Prime ribs. Creamed spinach. I decided to take a walk around the area. See the movie stars' homes. The police came again. "What are you doing out here?" they asked.

"I stay at this hotel. I am a guest of Universal Studios." They didn't care. They told me to shut up. Next thing I know I'm handcuffed to a tree. "You'll learn a lesson." They abandoned me for three hours. Motorists who were passing by began throwing beer cans at me. When they released me, I went back. I told the hotel manager, who calls Universal, who calls the Beverly Hill Police to apologize to me. They said, "You shouldn't have been out after 9." I called my mother. "Be right there. You stay where you are. I'll drive out there to get you." I told her to stay where she was. My agent called and said, "What are you going to do?" "I'm going to work." "That's what I expect you to do," he said. So I went to Universal. It took me forty-five minutes to get to the set because Security didn't believe that I was starring in a white production. That was my first twenty-four hours in Los Angeles.

ISHMAEL REED: *Let's back up. Basketball.*

LOU GOSSETT: I was invited to play with the New York Knicks. I was never drafted, but I was invited to the rookie camp.

ISHMAEL REED: *You said in Greenwich Village that there was some racism beneath the surface.*

LOU GOSSETT: Yeah there were people from everywhere. It was racist. It was subtle. It was all right to have long hair. Before the hippies there were the Beatniks. They came from Kansas and Oklahoma. Like Jack Kerouac and Lenny Bruce. You can't tell them to get rid of all of that stuff right away. They immersed themselves within the new society in the Village. You would feel racial tension in the different cafes down there. Cafe Wha, Café Bohemia. They had problems. So had we. It takes generations to get rid of prejudice on both sides. You could have gone to Harvard and got Phi Beta Kappa and still have racist ideas. Like the president of the United States.

ISHMAEL REED: *They didn't like interracial dating.*

LOU GOSSETT: They didn't like that worth a damn.

ISHMAEL REED: *Did you know Johnny Romero?*

LOU GOSSETT: Yeah.

ISHMAEL REED: *I saw him in Paris.*

LOU GOSSETT: Me, too. All right. That's another story. The girl pleaded for his life.

ISHMAEL REED: *He had an affair with Carmine DeSapio's daughter. This was very interesting. In your book, you talk about women who are sent by pimps to set up celebrities. I immediately thought of Lawrence Taylor and Tiger Woods.*

LOU GOSSETT: Yeah, there were a few of them. Richard Pryor, Darryl Strawberry, Jack Johnson, Joe Louis, all of whom were too big for their britches. It wasn't just racial. It was more than racial. Joe Namath was a target. Even today. These women are a step above high-class call girls. In Tiger Woods' case. They take in your secrets. Tiger Woods did a gentlemanly thing. Phil Mickelson's family was always there. He kisses his family and wife every time. Tiger's family is not always there. They should have been there. He's on the road. He is stuck because he's between a rock and a hard place.

ISHMAEL REED: *You talk about white actors with drugs and alcohol costing production time and money.*

LOU GOSSETT: Robert Downey, Jr. But I can't talk about that. Alec Baldwin drank.

ISHMAEL REED: *So there is a double standard.*

LOU GOSSETT: There's always a double standard. After I got an Oscar, I had to appear with a white actor in order to work. I had to give them money.

ISHMAEL REED: *You said that white men have their own club.*

LOU GOSSETT: It's unspoken. They've got their own language. One brings drugs from the studio. I can't say his name. He knows. He knows that I know. I'm kind enough not to say his name, but he knows who he is.

ISHMAEL REED: *What was it like working with Diana Sands?*

LOU GOSSETT: It was wonderful. She would cook for me and I would cook for her. We used to give each other massages. We did a love scene in *The Landlord* together. Hal Ashby began to stutter. "I don't know how to tell you this," he said and then tried to explain how our lips were "poking out at the camera." The camera was making the image of our African lips even larger, so much so that they filled the screen. This was because the movie was done in Panavision.

ISHMAEL REED: *What?*

LOU GOSSETT: As a result, we had to regulate our kiss to fit the lens of the camera. Something we never would have had to do in the theater.

ISHMAEL REED: *You had an affair with the Italian ambassador's daughter?*

LOU GOSSETT: She was the daughter of an Italian ambassador or envoy. He was at the United Nations. I'm not sure what he did. She saw me in *The Blacks*, by Jean Genet. She was a mixture of French and Italian and was sad from the disappointing relationship she had with her last lover. She'd had an abortion by some famous person. She and I did everything together. She moved out of her apartment without my knowing. I came home one day and the apartment was empty, including the furniture. She went crazy because she wanted to stay with me for the rest of her life. I found out that her parents were disappointed in her relationship with me because I was black.

They had taken her on their private jet to the Alps and put her in a convent. They felt the nuns would help her recover from being with me. She didn't want to go, which I didn't know until several years later. She came out a different person. She dropped her friends and insisted she was gay. I thought that I could change her. It never happened. Five years later we ran into each other. She had come to photograph a play I was in. She was no longer beautiful. She had grown heavy and bitter. She said to me, "Get away from me. I know what you did." I backed off. She did very well when it came to her photography. She was disappointed by three men, including her father.

ISHMAEL REED: *You did a film in Kenya and had an altercation.*

LOU GOSSETT: There was a pilot in Kenya from Rhodesia. At the time Rhodesia was like South Africa. Apartheid. Obstructionists were the Arabs, East Indians and the British who didn't want the transition from colony to independence. Jomo Kenyatta, Julius Nyerere. The only helicopter pilot was a white man from Rhodesia [now Zimbabwe]. The director wanted a scene where the helicopter was to brush by me. I jumped into a hole and the helicopter goes over my head. I remembered the helicopter. The helicopter hit my shoulder. The director said, "Great shot." The next thing you know I hit this guy, the pilot. I had him on the ground strangling him. I don't remember doing it. When the helicopter hit me, he was smiling. I got the photograph. I had never done that. I just lost it. It's like the scene where the mama sees the child under the car and she lifts up that car. I was going to kill him. He almost died.

ISHMAEL REED: *One passage in the book shows why some westerns are pro Confederate. "Shane," for example and the lionization of Confederate mass murderers, Frank and Jesse James. They hire Southerners to play cowboys. Some Southern extras left some excrement on the floor of your trailer. Gave you bad saddles. What did the producers say about this?*

LOU GOSSETT: The producers didn't know until after the fact. I did a film called *Cowboy in Africa* where I played the part as Fulah

Hemera, the African chief. It was filmed at Disney Ranch in Hollywood instead of in the mountains of Kenya. I took the role seriously. It was nighttime and thirty-seven degrees outside. It was 37 degrees. I was almost naked and freezing. I said to the director, "I think the chief should put on some animal skins. After all, this is his country, and he has been here longer than the cowboy. He is supposed to be a smart man who knows how to treat cows and practice animal husbandry. He'll look ridiculous standing here, shaking. Maybe you should give me some animal skins." The director said, "Action." I continued, "Wait a minute. Do you know how this is going to look to millions of viewers who will see a person who is not smart enough to dress properly? We'll lose all sense of authenticity. A chief would look ridiculous standing here, shaking…" He repeated, "Action." I said it a few more times and he still insisted: "Action!" A member of the crew told me later on, "Good job. We could have been there all night."

ISHMAEL REED: *So you got a reputation for being difficult?*

LOU GOSSETT: Yeah.

ISHMAEL REED: *What does it mean to be difficult?*

LOU GOSSETT: You speak your mind.

ISHMAEL REED: *You speak your mind?*

LOU GOSSETT: I speak my mind. This book would have come out two years later if I had spoken my mind. I'm making a comeback and so I had to be nice. You still have to exist.

ISHMAEL REED: *Black and white actors get paid, differently?*

LOU GOSSETT: I never made a million dollars in a movie.

ISHMAEL REED: *This is supposed to be liberal Hollywood. Progressive. They gave money to Obama.*

LOU GOSSETT: They are supposed to be working on that, but it has become a problem. There is automatic superiority about equality. We have to respect each other, and that's what we have to teach our children. Otherwise it will continue into the next generation and the next.

ISHMAEL REED: *You know Muhammad Ali?*

LOU GOSSETT: That was my buddy. We lived down the street from each other. We used to run together.

ISHMAEL REED: *What do you think of him lighting the Olympic torch?*

LOU GOSSETT: He said what I couldn't say. He said a lot of things that we couldn't say.

ISHMAEL REED: *You mean back in the '60s.*

LOU GOSSETT: Yeah.

ISHMAEL REED: *What about the endorsement of Reagan?*

LOU GOSSETT: It doesn't matter. It's all the same.

ISHMAEL REED: *When did you get married?*

LOU GOSSETT: I knew her six months before I got married. She had a complex about her from being terrorized, which is what happens to Mexican and Filipino women, which she took out on me. She got pregnant the first time we had sex. She had the baby and then disappeared with the baby.

ISHMAEL REED: *You said you calmed him down by playing Satie.*

LOU GOSSETT: You know the term crack baby? He was a hot sauce baby. He's my boy, six foot six. You know about my other son?

ISHMAEL REED: *Yeah. Beautiful family.*

LOU GOSSETT (Points to photos on the coffee table). That's his kids with his first wife. Then he married into another family. And here is my other son and his family. (Gossett adopted a child who was homeless.) He has a PhD.

ISHMAEL REED: *I wrote a piece about* Precious *in* The New York Times. *A lot of the people are disappointed with the movies coming out, like* American Gangster.

LOU GOSSETT: They gave Denzel Washington an Oscar for *Training Day*. He should have gotten one for *Malcolm X* or *Hurricane* or *The Great Debaters*.

ISHMAEL REED: *How were you able to take over the script for* An Officer and a Gentleman?

LOU GOSSETT: Me and my agent who grew up with me back in New York—named Ed Bondy—got the role of Sergeant Emil Foley for me, even though the role was for a white man. I'd played judges, a chief of police, an anthropologist. I had to do it 100 percent right because I had to whip my Marines into shape and bring them back up from scratch. I was in good shape from going into military life at Marine Corps Recruitment. They sent me twenty miles away.

ISHMAEL REED: *In the original script Gere beats up the Drill Sergeant.*

LOU GOSSETT: The Marines changed it. They said that an enlisted man would never beat up a Drill Sergeant. We'll tear the place up unless you change it. They said, "If you don't do this well, Mr. Gossett, we're going to have to kill you." The director was happy about that. The three of us should have received Oscars. Gere, the director and I.

ISHMAEL REED: *This woman Christiana who accused you of supplying your children with cereal laced with cocaine. Was she bi-polar?*

LOU GOSSETT: They believed her story.

ISHMAEL REED: *Why?*

LOU GOSSETT: Because I was black. What else would it be? They threw it out. The police officer lost his job. She never showed up to court and the newspapers never printed a retraction.

ISHMAEL REED: *Do you think you have a guardian angel? Here you are about to get evicted and a royalty check arrives on the day of the eviction. It's for a song you wrote for Richie Havens. Then this cocaine story is broadcast nationwide and just as things look bleak, you get an Oscar.*

LOU GOSSETT: I have a couple of guardian angels.

ISHMAEL REED: *Who told you that you had an Oscar?*

LOU GOSSETT: I'm still in shock. It's over there. (*Points to a shelf that holds the Oscar and other awards including Emmys, Golden Globes and People's Choice awards.*)

ISHMAEL REED: *There were several times when you got serious illnesses. Like in Mexico?*

LOU GOSSETT: Like when you drink the water and eat the salad? You get parasites. Yeah, we don't have strong immune systems in this country. We get sick when we leave the country. Others have it in their system. They don't get sick. We are antiseptic.

ISHMAEL REED: *And then you got the mold.*

LOU GOSSETT: That was here. I was on the road, hardly ever at home. There was a leak in the front door and the carpet got mildew. I came in and there was mold all on my furniture, it was damp. I got it cleaned up and went on the road again. Twenty years later it was in the wood and I'm inhaling and I got it in my lungs and my skin was itchy. I went to Canada to do a movie. I went to a doctor who treated me for it. They tested my blood. It could have killed me. The doctor said, "Do you realize how much mold you have in your blood?" I got massive doses of blood infusions and antibiotics. That was almost ten years ago.

ISHMAEL REED: *You said because you got sick, other people got roles that you could have gotten.*

LOU GOSSETT: Yeah. That's another story. I got acupuncture and they tore the original house down and redid it. There was mold everywhere. I had to live in a hotel and then the back house. It took a year. It gave me a new life. I was supposed to be out of here. I should have been out of here three or four times. But when I was appearing in *Lackawanna Blues* I was dying. I had to have the house torn down and rebuilt. It was the beginning of a new life. I've walked down that tunnel three or four times toward death only to be turned back.

ISHMAEL REED: *You talk about your friend Jon Voigt. He's a real right-winger.*

LOU GOSSETT: Well whatever he is he can be whatever he wants to be.

ISHMAEL REED: *He's one of these birthers.*

LOU GOSSETT: He's nuts.

ISHMAEL REED: *You were warned by producers to stay away from white women? I go to the movies and the white male actors can have any woman they want.*

LOU GOSSETT: God bless them.

ISHMAEL REED: *They get anyone they want. Whom are these movies for?*

LOU GOSSETT: They are for young white boys to give them strength and courage. They must need that. I get my power from God.

ISHMAEL REED: *You wanted to do a series on the Harlem Renaissance. I want to know the name of the writer who agreed to do it.*

LOU GOSSETT: I won't give out his name. It's too much pressure on him. It's embarrassing to ask HBO to do this.

ISHMAEL REED: *They do* The Wire. *You were in two movies with Tyler Perry. What do you think about Spike Lee calling his movies "coonery and buffoonery?"*

LOU GOSSETT: I think Spike Lee is frustrated. He should leave the brother alone.

ISHMAEL REED: *Why do you think he's frustrated?*

LOU GOSSETT: Because he is a brilliant man and he's got a complex. He should leave the anger alone. He'll get there. Right now he's in a hurry.

ISHMAEL REED: *Did you see* Miracle at Saint Anna?

LOU GOSSETT: Brilliant. *Malcolm X* was brilliant. He has to calm down and he'll be OK.

ISHMAEL REED: *I want to end with you talking about racism.*

LOU GOSSETT: I feel like we should all get along and in order to do that we have to get rid of thinking about what happened in the past. We have to start with God being in charge. We need self respect, respect for our elders, respect for the opposite sex, our dress code, how we conduct ourselves, how we talk, our country, conflict resolution. The stuff that makes us ladies and gentleman is gone. "Scarface," or wherever they got it from, they got it. The children are brilliant but they need to change their attitudes. They have to get a positive attitude. The streets need to get safer. The kids have to be taught who they really are. The difference between Michael Johnson and Michael Vick. One had a foundation, one didn't.

ISHMAEL REED: *Do you believe in the Rapture? (I was referring to a movie called* Left Behind, *a Christian movie, in which Gossett plays the president of the United States.)*

LOU GOSSETT: I try not to think about it, but yeah. The second coming is happening because we think that we are in charge. The oil spills, the tsunami, and the earthquakes are a sign. Those of us who look toward the light will be here. Those who don't will be gone.

At Work: Ishmael Reed on *Juice!*[1]

PARIS REVIEW: Juice! *is your first novel since 1993. What inspired you to write another novel after all these years?*

ISHMAEL REED: I began this one as soon as I heard about the murders. I was vacationing in Hawaii, and the murders ruined my vacation. The media went berserk over the murder of Nicole Simpson, the kind of ideal white woman—a Rhine maiden—one finds in Nazi art and propaganda, murdered allegedly by a black beast. It was a story that reached into the viscera of the American unconscious, recalling the old Confederate art of the black boogeyman as an incubus squatting on top of a sleeping, half-clad white woman. It was also an example of collective blame. All black men became O. J. The murders ignited a kind of hysteria.

PARIS REVIEW: Juice! *does not have a conventional structure. The novel incorporates courtroom documents, television transcripts, and pieces of visual art. It also plays around quite a bit with time. What gave rise to the novel's peculiar shape?*

ISHMAEL REED: I try to experiment. Writing a conventional novel would be boring for me. In this novel, I added cartoons. Cartoons were probably my introduction to storytelling as a child, because on Sundays we got *The Chattanooga Times*, and I'd read the funnies. A publisher

---

1. *J.D. Mitchell conducted this interview published in* The Paris Review *on September 13, 2011.* Juice!, *published by Dalkey Archive in April 2011, tells the story of a struggling African American cartoonist whose personal and professional life is disrupted by the media frenzy surrounding the O. J. Simpson murder trial.*

wanted to publish *Juice!* but decided that the cartoons weren't up to par. So, at the age of seventy, I studied at the Cartoon Art Museum of San Francisco, and the cartoons improved so much that I now do political cartoons for *The San Francisco Chronicle's* blog, City Brights.

PARIS REVIEW: *Both* Juice! *and your previous novel* Japanese by Spring *focus on people of color desperately seeking acceptance from predominantly white institutions. Is the topic of tokenism informed by your early years in the New York literary world?*

ISHMAEL REED: Absolutely. When the old *Saturday Review of Literature* anointed me the number one token, I wrote a letter telling them that I was not, which, as far as I know, was unprecedented. White New Yorkers have had a great influence over which black writer is divo or diva since at least the 1920s. At one time, the Communist Party had the influence. When Chester Himes and Richard Wright broke with the party, it was the end of their careers in the United States. In the 1960s, when black nationalism was in vogue, all black characters had to be portrayed in a positive way, and when the feminist movement was born out of black nationalism, so did all black women. Since the mid-1970s, white feminists have had great influence over which black fiction gets marketed. I've gotten a lot of heat from some women in parts of academia, publishing, and book reviewing. On some occasions, they've censored my work. The late Joe Wood asked me to write a piece about Oakland politics for *The Village Voice.* He said that a feminist editor at the time wouldn't even read it on the grounds that I was a "notorious sexist."

I've also been called paranoid for including in *Reckless Eyeballing* a white feminist character named Becky French who is in the business of manufacturing black divas and black boogeyman melodramas. Toni Morrison, Michele Wallace and bell hooks have made similar comments about white feminists directing trends in black literature, yet nobody calls them paranoid.

PARIS REVIEW: *When you first began writing in the sixties, African-American literature was not really a respected tradition. Do you think the situation for black writers has improved since then?*

ISHMAEL REED: Black male literature, classically, the literature of dissent reaching back to David Walker's *Appeal* (1829), has been murdered. Some members of the younger black male avant-garde have gone to Germany for recognition. When the great John Edgar Wideman can only get a book published by a vanity press, then you know that all of us are in trouble (except for those who write that the slave masters were black, or that the problems of black Americans are self-inflicted, the kind of stuff that excites the Pulitzer and Tony juries). The Kindle, Nook, and iPad might change this, because soon we will be able to download the work of black writers in Asia, Africa, and Europe, where the atmosphere is not as hostile as it is here.

I've managed to survive because I write poetry, plays, and songs as well as fiction. My income is supplemented by royalties from poetry and songs. Within the last few months, I've written songs for Macy Gray and the rapper Black Thought. When Tupac mentioned me in a song, it compensated for all of the hostile responses to my nonfiction and fiction.

PARIS REVIEW: *The legacy of Ralph Ellison looms large in the world of African-American letters. The two of you are perhaps the only black American male writers to enjoy such longevity and critical attention. Did Ellison influence your work?*

ISHMAEL REED: Ellison looms large because *Invisible Man* is one of a few books by black men and women that white academics and reviewers are acquainted with. I didn't read Ellison until 1968, when I used *Invisible Man* in a classroom. There were many influences on my early work, some of them from painting and music. If I had to point to a black writer who influenced my first novel, *The Free Lance Pallbearers*, it would be Charles Wright, who wrote *The Wig*. James Weldon Johnson, Chester Himes, Zora Neale Hurston, and Rudolph Fisher were among my black influences. But the main influence on my second and third novels was Joe Overstreet, who introduced me to the sophistication of African religion and its ability to soak up different traditions. I think that my work has more in common with that of Romare Bearden and the Saar women, Lezley and Betye Saar, than with writers.

I think that the accusations that Ellison was an Uncle Tom are unfair. I understood this after I read Arnold Rampersad's biography. Ellison experienced the aftermath of the Tulsa Riot of 1921 and probably suffered post-traumatic stress from that experience. Three hundred black people were massacred. It showed that some whites resort to savagery when hopped up on the social heroin of racism. Then Ellison had to make compromises during the period of the Red Scare, and abandon his Communist politics. He had to cut down the competition so that he could remain number one and, even with all of his honors, he was humiliated. When he finally broke with his patrons, they abandoned him. A sad, sad story.

PARIS REVIEW: *Are you optimistic about the survival of traditional African-American folk culture?*

ISHMAEL REED: I think that the use of African-American folklore comes in cycles, when there is a need for its renewal. The source for hip-hop is folklore. The features one finds in hip-hop can be found in the old "toasts" that arose from the criminal underworld. Cecil Brown in his book *Stagolee* covers some of this, as do Sterling Brown, Quincy Troupe, Steve Cannon, and Colson Whitehead. But now I'm looking at Native American folklore and beginning to look at Southwestern magical realism, which existed before the South American version. I even found a Shango, the Nigerian "saint" associated with thunder, in a story from the Southwest.

THE RETURN OF THE NIGGER BREAKERS: A GHETTO READING AND WRITING RAT RESPONDS TO HIS CRITICS[1]

Jill Nelson Interviews Ishmael Reed

Barack Obama and the Jim Crow Media, The Return of the Nigger Breakers (Baraka Books) is Reed's fourth book of media criticism. We talked to Reed while he was on the East Coast on a brief tour to promote a book whose publication and scathing critique of racist, corporate controlled media has largely and not surprisingly been ignored by those whom Reed labels the "Jim Crow Media."

JILL NELSON: *Your latest book was published last month. Would you explain its sub-title: "The Return of the Nigger Breakers"?*

ISHMAEL REED: Edward Covey was a member of a profession whose job was to tame unruly slaves. Frederick Douglass was one of those men who was sent to him, a Nigger Breaker, to be disciplined. Douglass turned the tables on him and thrashed him. I argue that this is the aim of the media, and other institutions that are opposed to Obama. Moreover, with the firing and buyouts of hundreds of minority journalists, black institutions, blacks in general, black

---

1. A version of this interview appeared at the website *The Defenders On Line* on May 14, 2010.

celebrities and even the president are being judged by a mostly white media and a handful of acceptable right-wing blacks, a few of whom are farther to the right than the white right.

JILL NELSON: *The book was published by a Canadian-based publisher. Why were you unable to get this book published in the United States?*

ISHMAEL REED: This is attributable to the state of black letters. Serious fiction and non-fiction by blacks are becoming extinct, except for those which uphold the current line coming from the media owners and the corporations: that all of the problems of Africans and African Americans are due to their behavior. Terry McMillan, interviewed in the Spring 2010 issue of *Konch* (IshmaelReedpub.com) says that black fiction that is selling is urban fiction that shows blacks at their worst. This is not to say that black criminals don't exist. But that's all we get from the mainstream media, television and movies. This is true not only for literature but for theater, film, art galleries and opinion columns as well.

At one time, blacks could respond through writing. James Baldwin served as a diamond megaphone for black aspirations and could debate critics of black people one on one. But with the disappearance of serious black fiction and non-fiction, this is no longer the case. Now this book, which my agent said no American publisher would publish, was published in Quebec. Between April 14 and 20, I did national media in Canada with front page stories in the major dailies and weeklies, a front page story in *The Montreal Review of Books* and was greeted by crowds in Montreal and Toronto. In Montreal, they had to turn people away. This must have been what it was like when the fugitive slaves traveled abroad and lectured. My advice to young writers is that they seek audiences elsewhere. It's a big world.

JILL NELSON: *Much of your recent work has focused on media criticism. Why?*

ISHMAEL REED: The segregated American media with its alliance with the right wing and racist forces like the tea party movement—

which was created, organized, and amplified by the segregated Jim Crow media—are the most powerful opponents to black and Hispanic progress. It's not surprising that they have, using the late Carl Rowan's expression, "outpropagandized" blacks and white Democrats and progressives as well. That's because they have billions at their disposal.

The insurance companies put $350 million out to defeat health care reform and bankrolled this faux grassroots movement, which is white men, among the most privileged groups in world history. The media have overblown the strength of this movement because racism is big business for them. The coverage of a gun rally that was held near Washington, D.C., on April 19 was typical. CNN didn't do aerial shots because that would have revealed the small turnout. The media are the mob leaders. And they cater to a niche of people who are addicted to the need to believe in black pathology.

JILL NELSON: *On that point, you wrote very critically about the movie* Precious, *and took a good deal of heat for it. Did you feel compelled to speak out?*

ISHMAEL REED: Most of the responses I received from whites and black men and women were 85 percent positive. This propaganda movie had to be challenged because powerful critics were saying that this family was the typical black family living in poverty. I never denied that child abuse occurs in American communities. What the supporters of this movie were suggesting is that incest is "prevalent" in African-American communities! And the media line was that only a few black angry men were opposed to the movie. I pointed out that a number of black women and even white women intellectuals spoke out against the film. In fact, a recent issue of my zine *Konch* publishes two articles written by white women who are vociferous in their opposition to the movie. Thirty years from now, *Precious* will seem like an odd throwback to the days when blacks were shown running away from the farmer's shotgun with chickens in both hands.

JILL NELSON: *Ishmael, your information about the media seems encyclopedic. What do you read, watch, listen to, what sites on the internet?*

ISHMAEL REED: I read three newspapers each day, where the typical portrait of a black man has him in an orange jumpsuit. I watch cable and monitor the opinion pages whose post-race line is usually challenged by reports and studies printed in the same newspapers. I do not come to criticism of the media empty-handed.

JILL NELSON: *Any advice on how to become more critical in news consumption?*

ISHMAEL REED: I have an online magazine. I get useful information each day from those who write on Facebook, *Counterpunch.com*, *Media Matters*, *FAIR*. And Richard Prince's "Journalisms" are essential.

JILL NELSON: *Do you think technology, particularly the Internet, is loosening the grip of corporate media?*

ISHMAEL REED: Yes, that's why they're trying control it.

JILL NELSON: *Given your analysis in the "Jim Crow Media," how do people of color, progressives and others critique Barack Obama without colluding with corporate America's agenda?*

ISHMAEL REED: I have some problems with some of Obama's policies, but as long as these people are threatening to kill him and his family, and calling his mother, a distinguished Irish-American anthropologist, "white trash" and even worse, I'm on his side. All of the stored-up bile of white supremacy has exploded like airborne E-Coli as a result of Obama's election. One Republican site just put up a photo depicting Obama and Michelle as characters in *Sanford and Son*. He's not only the nation's president but he's also its chief exorcist, like a St. Patrick stoking the nation's lizard brain.

The progressives are uncomfortable with Obama because they've been opposed to black leadership, historically. The progressive media is just as segregated as the corporate media, which they are always criticizing from their glass houses. Richard Prince printed a photo of a Huffington Post Xmas party. One black staffer!! The opposition to Obama from people of color comes from the fringes. He has a 90 percent approval rating from blacks, over 60 percent from Hispanics and he carried the Asian-American vote. Yet these arrogant white progressives say they are his base and that he is obligated to them.

JILL NELSON: *Where do you think American media will be in five or ten years?*

ISHMAEL REED: Newspapers will be dead and buried and maybe some enterprising scholar will write a book about how they fomented racial and civil strife and helped the American government justify useless wars since the 1830s. Mao [Zedong] had a habit of sending intellectuals among the peasants from time to time so that they might understand what's what. That's what should happen with the "tough-lovers" and post-race entrepreneurs at Yale, Harvard and the Think Tanks. Send them to live in Detroit, Oakland, or Washington D.C. inner cities for a couple of years. See what happens. See what happens.

Jill Nelson is a journalist and author of five books. She lectures widely on race, gender, politics and media.

An Interview
with Terry McMillan[1]

ISHMAEL REED: *Have you read* The Help *by Kathryn Stockett?*

TERRY MCMILLAN: She can write. I'm reading it. I bought it.

ISHMAEL REED: *Well, she's got fresh material about how white women in the South think about black women.*

TERRY MCMILLAN: I have a problem with that book.

ISHMAEL REED: *The dialect? Is it pretty bad?*

TERRY MCMILLAN: When white people read it, they think it is "spot on" as they would say. Not only that, but what really annoyed me is when a white person writes a book from black characters' points of view it gets on the best sellers list. Then you have black people writing about the same thing and they can't get a deal. They can't get a book contract. People who are writing about our world and our lives. I mean I give the girl [Stockett] credit because it is brave what she did.

ISHMAEL REED: *Well, let me ask you something. Do the critics know the difference between the fake and what's real?*

TERRY MCMILLAN: What do you mean?

ISHMAEL REED: Times' *critic Michiko Kakutani fell for this fake book,* Love and Consequences *by Margaret Seltzer, about how the author*

---

1. A version of this interview conducted by Ishmael Reed and Tennessee Reed was published in Konch Magazine at Ishmaelreedpublishing.com in spring 2010.

grew up in a gang environment. The author got a $100,000 advance.
Michiko Kakutani gave it a rave.

TERRY MCMILLAN: And they found out she made it all up. That's
what I'm trying to say. I read the first forty pages of *The Help*. As a
black writer, I wouldn't think of writing a book with that title. My
agent asked me, "Terry, are you going to read *The Help*?" I couldn't
read the book. It wouldn't even work. I wonder why white people
who deal with black characters for the most part don't even have
pictures of black people on the cover? In *The Help* you got birds. In
The Secret Life of Bees you got bees when most of the characters are
black. When my next book comes out I'm going to have birds and
bees on the cover.

ISHMAEL REED: *So what are you working on now?*

TERRY MCMILLAN: I just finished a book.

ISHMAEL REED: *What is it about?*

TERRY MCMILLAN: It is about the women from *Waiting to Exhale*
fifteen years later. (*Getting To Happy* was published in September
2010.) The women are in their fifties. It was kind of by accident. I
didn't do it intentionally.

ISHMAEL REED: *So, what's happening with them?*

TERRY MCMILLAN: *The women?*

ISHMAEL REED: *Yeah.*

TERRY MCMILLAN: They are dealing with real life issues.

ISHMAEL REED: *Like what?*

TERRY MCMILLAN: Many. They are dealing with various forms of
loss. One woman loses her husband. One woman has never been
married and she is a single mother. One woman lost her job after
eighteen years of employment and she was kicked to the curb. She
doesn't think she will find another man. Another one was conned
by her second husband years ago.

ISHMAEL REED: *How did he con her?*

TERRY MCMILLAN: He was already married to somebody else. He pretended to be a civil rights attorney. He was living a double life. His other wife was the one who busted him. Let her know. She had difficulty getting over it and so she started popping pills to deal with it. One of them is dealing with a marriage—she didn't get married until forty-two or something like that, and she married a really cool guy, but he was boring. She has to decide at fifty-one or whatever to get a divorce, but her family thinks it is stupid at fifty-one years of age to be running around. "You ain't Beyoncé, honey," they say. But she does it, anyway. But it's kind of cool and it's sort of what they've had to learn what to do, making adjustments in their lives.

ISHMAEL REED: *Are these middle-class women?*

TERRY MCMILLAN: Yeah. The one who got conned, her husband kind of took her to the cleaners, so she is in trouble. She doesn't want her friends to know. She doesn't want everybody to know.

ISHMAEL REED: *That she has downsized?*

TERRY MCMILLAN: Well, she has already downsized.

ISHMAEL REED: *How?*

TERRY MCMILLAN: No more BMWs.

TENNESSEE REED: *A Hoopty?*

TERRY MCMILLAN: No. She has an eight-year-old Tahoe or something like that.

ISHMAEL REED: *How do her friends treat her?*

TERRY MCMILLAN: They don't treat her any different. They know that she is going through something, though. She is going to rehab. She doesn't really want their help because they are all going through something. They are middle class. They aren't rich.

TENNESSEE REED: *What about the woman who had the heart attack?*

TERRY MCMILLAN: That's Gloria.

TENNESSEE REED: *What about the one who had the gay husband?*

TERRY MCMILLAN: I think that was Gloria. He's not in this book.

ISHMAEL REED: *How many characters do you have in this book?*

TERRY MCMILLAN: Probably about six, seven. They have kids. They have teenage daughters. One is a mixed child. I mean it just worked out this way.

ISHMAEL REED: *I saw this movie by Tyler Perry called* Meet the Browns. *Angela Bassett was in there. Why would they have these stereotypical characters? Like* Precious. *Angela Bassett is a great actor.*

TERRY MCMILLAN: She needed the paycheck.

ISHMAEL REED: Precious *was marketed to whites, too.*

TERRY MCMILLAN: Of course it was.

ISHMAEL REED: *They wrote off the black market.*

TERRY MCMILLAN: They didn't care. I know a lot of black people who refused to see that film. I didn't want to see it because I remember the book and I had respect for Sapphire as a poet; I read with her in London.

ISHMAEL REED: *What kind of reception did she get in London?*

TERRY MCMILLAN: She scared the daylights out of everybody. She was angry.

ISHMAEL REED: *She got $500,000 from Knopf. They published* Push *and* American Dream. *The people who did* Precious *were inspired by* The Color Purple. *They took it a step further. The mother is a pedophile.*

TERRY MCMILLAN: Well, all I can say is that it is disturbing and it really makes me angry.

Ishmael Reed: *The 90s was the decade when black people bought a lot of books. What happened?*

TERRY MCMILLAN: Well, people didn't want to buy all of that ghetto stuff.

ISHMAEL REED: *What gangbanging? Urban fiction? Chic Lit?*

TERRY MCMILLAN: Same thing.

ISHMAEL REED: *Did they get a lot of money?*

TERRY MCMILLAN: No. It was quite the opposite. Some of them self publish.

ISHMAEL REED: *None of them got money?*

TERRY MCMILLAN: I'm talking about before urban ghetto victimization. People changed that. It's almost like writers are being pimped. You had a lot of people right out of prison writing their own stories and others who got out of prison and started their own publishing companies. Unfortunately, none of them knew anything about editing, so you had these poorly written books. They still are. Some of them have gotten better, but they still glorify—it's almost the opposite of films and books like *Push*—I mean they glorify violence and sex; people get killed. Murdered. There are just so many ways you can give a blow job, but every other page is someone on a pole, and somebody is doing this or that. They are trying to become more professional, but there are so many of them, they cancel each other out.

ISHMAEL REED: *Do people buy these books?*

TERRY MCMILLAN: Some do, but not as many as people think. I remember seeing a Barnes & Noble on 6th Avenue and 22nd Street in New York. They would pull up in their trucks and sell them right in front of the store. They would sell those books; who liked them? White men. There's nothing but naked black women on the cover. They love the cover of these books. Every single one of them has nothing but black women showing all of their body. They don't have on any clothes. That's what got on my nerves. Even at Barnes & Noble, at the end of each aisle, they had them all stacked up.

ISHMAEL REED: *Well, they are black porno. Porno and violence.*

TERRY MCMILLAN: That's it. Some of them live in the Bay Area. I'm not saying any names.

ISHMAEL REED: *When Blanche (Blanche Richardson, manager of Marcus Bookstore in Oakland) got robbed they stole those books. They stole those kinds of books. All of these black bookstores are in trouble.*

TERRY MCMILLAN: I tried to help them as much as I could. Over the years.

ISHMAEL REED: *Yeah, I know.*

TERRY MCMILLAN: No, you don't know. And now it is just really bad. People think it's the economy. I don't think it's the economy. I think part of it is a backlash. All of these publishers are owned by damn near the same company with all of these buyouts and takeovers and all of this and when they clamp down, they change their plans. They let people go, and back during *Waiting to Exhale,* there weren't enough bookstores. There were three in New York City and there was Emma Roberts down in Dallas. They are all in trouble. I try to help out as much as I can.

ISHMAEL REED: *Where do you think people spend their money?*

TERRY MCMILLAN: Gas, electricity, and the Depression.

ISHMAEL REED: *We have a black president.*

TERRY MCMILLAN: Yeah, I know we have a black president, but he's not a magician. I don't want to get on Barack Obama today because I have a lot of respect for him. I don't care what anybody else says.

ISHMAEL REED: *Have you met him?*

TERRY MCMILLAN: Yeah.

ISHMAEL REED: *What is your impression of him?*

TERRY MCMILLAN: I like him. I think he's brilliant. I think he's very smart and he gets it. I think he's an idealist and he took on burdens that someone else had created. The country was screwed up when he came into office. They couldn't pick a better time for a black man to come into office to be president.

ISHMAEL REED: *He saved them from a Depression.*

TERRY MCMILLAN: And he's going to save them from a lot more.

ISHMAEL REED: *These progressives are worse than the right wing.*

TERRY MCMILLAN: I saw Danny Glover opening up his big mouth.

ISHMAEL REED: *The Academy of Motion Picture establishment is white. Why can't he change that? Why can't Danny Glover, Denzel Washington and Samuel Jackson change that?*

TERRY MCMILLAN: I don't know; I think that I pissed my agent off. She asked me about *The Help* and I went off on her. She was surprised. I said, "It's racist. The same thing is happening in publishing. It's just not about me." I explained to her that *The Help* was right up there with *Push*. When we show our pathology white people get a kick out of it. They see it as art. But write about struggling to pay the rent or we have the same struggles as everybody else, and that's boring. We want to tell our own stories and the industry doesn't want to embrace it. You know, I see a lot of hypocrisy out here, you know. I do not need anybody pointing out to me the hypocrisy. *The Help* is about guilt about black nannies taking care of white babies. Who better than a white person to write this? White people like the book. Black people are offended by it. There's going to be a movie.

ISHMAEL REED: *What? Which black actor would perform in such a movie? Who wants to see such a movie?*

TERRY MCMILLAN: You'll see. Anybody who is behind in their mortgage. They just bought movie rights for my new book. The big thing is, because people assume I know these actors, "Can you get me a…" and I say, "No, I don't talk to those people." A lot of what is important to them is not important to me.

ISHMAEL REED: *What is important to them?*

TERRY MCMILLAN: Getting a movie role. I can't speak for everybody, but they don't have any roles. Just like in publishing. A lot of this stuff doesn't make sense. I'm not buying it. When I saw *Precious* I complained. I said I couldn't think of a single black mother who would treat her children that way or watch their daughter raped, sodomized or whatever by her boyfriend. That's just unrealistic. And I know people who have been abused all kinds of ways. This film took it too far. Her mother throws frying pans at her and tells her she ain't shit. Sapphire stockpiled all of the stories that she heard when she worked in one of these places. She took these characters and put them all under one roof. I know some people are abused. Sapphire looks scary to me. I'll put it this way. I don't even know how to say this, but I wanted to walk out of that movie quite a few times.

ISHMAEL REED: *How many people were present at the theater when you saw it?*

TERRY MCMILLAN: Not many. I said, you know what, every stereotype, a little girl—black obese girl from the ghetto, who is illiterate, with a Mongoloid child. She walks away with two babies. She has AIDS. And she's walking off into the sunset. She went around the corner to another project. Everybody who helped save her was of mixed race, or white. I have nothing against biracial people.

MUSICIAN AND COMPOSER
WITHOUT BORDERS

An Interview with David Murray[1]

Ishmael Reed interviews saxophonist/composer David Murray and his wife, Valerie, on Murray's early years in music. This interview took place on October 10, 2009, in Oakland, California.

ISHMAEL REED: *Let's talk about 3-D Family Agency.*

DAVID MURRAY: The 3-D Family Agency? Okay.

ISHMAEL REED: *What inspired you to start working with African and Caribbean musicians?*

DAVID MURRAY: What inspired me? Personally?

ISHMAEL REED: *Yeah. When did it begin?*

DAVID MURRAY: Well, when I left New York and I came over to Paris, I guess that must have been thirteen years ago. That was the moment.

---

1. A version of this interview first appeared in *Black Renaissance/Renaissance noire* on April 1, 2011. David Murray and Ishmael Reed have been collaborators since 1983, when David Murray, Taj Mahal, Steve Lacy, Allen Toussaint, Carman Moore and Carla Bley set Reed's songs and poetry to music for the CD *Conjure*, which took its title from Reed's second book of poetry. Since then the Conjure group has traveled to Europe and Japan. Their most recent collaborations include two songs written by Reed, set to music by Murray and performed by Cassandra Wilson on the CD *Sacred Ground*. The CD *The Devil Tried to Kill Me* appeared with two songs by Reed sung by Sista Kee and Taj Mahal in November of 2009. This interview took place at Reed's Oakland home in May of 2009.

ISHMAEL REED: *What year was that?*

DAVID MURRAY: 1996.

ISHMAEL REED: *Why did you leave New York?*

DAVID MURRAY: There were several things. My record contract had just finished; Bob Thiel had died. I was under a contract with Impube, but it was called Red Baron at the time. I was supposed to be in the studio on the day he passed. That was my big money record contract. Regarding living in New York, I guess that was it for me because I didn't want to get in no rat race, trying to get money in NYC—it's just too hard. The way these kids are now! These days they will do anything for a record. They will even pay to do a record.

ISHMAEL REED: *Are you talking about the hip-hoppers?*

DAVID MURRAY: I am talking about the jazz musicians in New York.

ISHMAEL REED: *Who are some of the young jazz musicians you are listening to?*

DAVID MURRAY: I just hear people in passing. Yesterday I heard Abraham Burton.

ISHMAEL REED: *What does he play?*

DAVID MURRAY: He plays tenor.

ISHMAEL REED: *Is he in Oakland?*

DAVID MURRAY: No. He played yesterday at the Malcolm X festival. I listen to people like James Carter who is about forty now. But you asked me about why I left New York and my point is that I left New York because I also met Valerie in Paris. We started working together.

ISHMAEL REED: *1995?*

DAVID MURRAY: Yeah.

ISHMAEL REED: *Under what circumstances?*

DAVID MURRAY: Well, she brought me over to France to do some concerts. She was working for *Banlieues Bleues*, which is the biggest jazz festival in France. She was the second person in command there and she was involved with fourteen cities, maybe even more.

ISHMAEL REED: *Did you do a tour?*

DAVID MURRAY: No, no. She ran social programs. She was in charge of all of these young—

ISHMAEL REED: *Fourteen cities?*

VALERIE MURRAY: Yes, we were working with young kids mostly from Africa: Nigerian kids, Senegalese kids, Tunisian-French kids, you know, all kinds of teenagers.

ISHMAEL REED: *Were there workshops for various instruments?*

VALERIE MURRAY: Yes. We organized lots of drum workshops. We used the ka drums. That was important to me. Everybody knows the Congas, but in France they don't know the Gwo-ka and the Ka drum, which is played mainly in Guadeloupe. One of the goals was to bring the drumming traditions of Guadeloupe to the kids living in France. It is important.

DAVID MURRAY: Yeah, exactly, because the Ka drum itself was on the slave ships. It was used as a container for salted meat, the only food for the captured Africans. They eventually put skin on these containers and created the Ka drums, creating music that channels their misery through Gwo-ka.

VALERIE MURRAY: The French try to erase this relationship to slavery from their memory. The overall attitude and general judgment towards their former involvement in slavery is hard.

ISHMAEL REED: *You mean they are denying this? They are erasing this from their memory?*

VALERIE MURRAY: For a long time most people used to. Now it's coming out. As David was saying, the parents don't want their kids to speak Creole in the house because it evokes memory of slave time.

DAVID MURRAY (*pointing to his shirt*): This shirt is in Creole. The guy who made this shirt had to do nine years in prison because he blew up part of an electrical company. He was one of the best artists in Guadeloupe. French people see this and they have no idea what it says because they don't speak Creole. They get mad when you speak Creole.

ISHMAEL REED: *So how many times have you been to Guadeloupe?*

VALERIE MURRAY: My sister lives there and I've been there a lot.

ISHMAEL REED: *Have you recorded there?*

DAVID MURRAY: Yeah, we recorded *The Devil Tried to Kill Me* there.

VALERIE MURRAY: They're having an insurrection there. They use the Gwo-Ka drums as a symbol.

DAVID MURRAY: They have this big group called the Akiyo. They have their own parade every year. Let me just say that the kids come out first, equipped with whips; they snap them. Bop, bop. That's the first line. In the second line, the Akio and behind them, the musicians. Then come the singers and dancers. It is big.

VALERIE MURRAY: Their outfits are incredible. Amazing, especially because everything is twenty percent more expensive than in France. Despite the immense struggles, they create incredible fashion and it goes with Gwo-ka drums.

ISHMAEL REED: *Like hip-hop in the States?*

VALERIE MURRAY: Yeah, I think so.

ISHMAEL REED: *So, David, what made you become an international musician while all of these other people are scrounging around places like New York, trying to get gigs?*

DAVID MURRAY: You know, when I left New York I felt like I had pretty much accomplished what I could have accomplished at that time. I was just finishing a deal with a major company and, like I said, Bob Thiel had passed away. My agreement with Valerie was to work together in Paris and try to maintain my international acclaim.

I left New York to become a citizen of the world, which is what I feel like today. I didn't want to be just a New York guy, another New York musician. I was getting into big band octets and larger projects.

ISHMAEL REED: *So, what's the situation for musicians in the United States right now?*

DAVID MURRAY: Well, I didn't want to end up living in New York with a police lock on my door and a bathroom in my kitchen, saying, "I made it in New York as a jazz musician." To me that wasn't the success I had imagined when I left Oakland, when I left Berkeley.

ISHMAEL REED: *When did you leave Berkeley?*

DAVID MURRAY: In March 1975. I said goodbye to my father and left.

ISHMAEL REED: *Why?*

DAVID MURRAY: Because I wanted to make it in New York and I was in college.

ISHMAEL REED: *Which college?*

DAVID MURRAY: Pomona College. That's when I met you in Malibu, we went to that film festival and I also knew already that going to Pomona College wasn't exactly what I wanted to do. I went there for a year and a half and then I got an independent study and went to New York with it. That's how I got to New York.

ISHMAEL REED: *What was the independent study?*

DAVID MURRAY: To research the saxophone since Ornette Coleman came to New York. I wanted to interview a lot of people.

ISHMAEL REED: *You had access to Coleman?*

DAVID MURRAY: Yes, I met Ornette Coleman because I knew Bobby Bradford who had played with him and John Carter. They were all from Fort Worth. I interviewed him. He knew who I was. He was the first person I interviewed because he knew Bobby Bradford closely.

ISHMAEL REED: *This was when you went to New York in 1975?*

DAVID MURRAY: Yeah, and I had met Arthur Blythe a year and a half before, so I was following him.

ISHMAEL REED: *Your mother played piano?*

DAVID MURRAY: Yes, my mother played piano.

ISHMAEL REED: *What was her name?*

DAVID MURRAY: Catherine Murray. She played at Ephesians Church around the corner from here.

ISHMAEL REED: *Ephesians is still there?*

DAVID MURRAY: Ephesians is still there. On Alcatraz. The Ephesians Church of God in Christ.

ISHMAEL REED: *How long?*

DAVID MURRAY: Not a long time. She met my father there. After that, she began playing at Fresno Temple where she was from. My grandfather was a sharecropper in Fresno, California.

ISHMAEL REED: *Where did he start out?*

DAVID MURRAY: He came out to California from Oklahoma City. He passed Fresno and came up to the Bay Area, didn't see cotton, so he returned to Fresno because he couldn't make a living.

ISHMAEL REED: *Was he part of the Black Exodus to the West?*

DAVID MURRAY: Exactly. He was lucky because he had mineral rights due to some oil he found in Texas, so he had some cash and he bought some property called Hackett Flats, which is located in Fresno. We still own it.

ISHMAEL REED: *What is Hackett Flats?*

DAVID MURRAY: Hackett Flats is almost a square mile of property. He was sharecropping there and organized people. I remember taking walks with him when he would go around the neighborhood. He would distribute food, like frozen meat, to different people.

ISHMAEL REED: *So was he a leader in the community?*

DAVID MURRAY: Yeah, he would tell the young men to get up and get on the truck. People got on the flatbed truck and he took them out to the cotton fields or they would go and pick grapes and any other crop.

ISHMAEL REED: *Were there many Mexicans as well?*

DAVID MURRAY: They came a little later. We couldn't pick as fast as the Mexicans. (*Laughter*). Basically, we used to fight the Mexicans.

ISHMAEL REED: *What do you mean you used to fight them?*

DAVID MURRAY: It wasn't like now with Brown Power, Black Power, we're all together. It wasn't like that in the early 1960s.

ISHMAEL REED: *Before the revolution?*

DAVID MURRAY: Yeah, before Viva La Raza; we were all local. Sometimes, blacks and Mexicans would get into fights.

ISHMAEL REED: *Was this over women?*

DAVID MURRAY: Sometimes over women, sometimes over territory and sometimes over skin color. Meanwhile, "the white man" loves it when colored people fight.

ISHMAEL REED: *What kind of music did you like when you were a kid?*

DAVID MURRAY: I grew up playing gospel.

ISHMAEL REED: *You still have that gospel tinge. You get "happy" and in Pentecostal terms, getting "happy" means becoming possessed.*

DAVID MURRAY: You're right, I remember Phil Hartman, who was a big teacher in the Berkeley Public School system. He was the cat who handed me my first alto saxophone.

ISHMAEL REED: *Is he still there?*

DAVID MURRAY: He is dead now, but he was the one who brought jazz to the Berkeley Public School system. He was my elementary school teacher. Man, he inspired me.

ISHMAEL REED: *Was there any resistance to his teaching jazz?*

DAVID MURRAY: Well, yeah, the school district wanted to teach classical music and concert band.

ISHMAEL REED: *What year was this?*

DAVID MURRAY: Well, I was nine. It had to be 1964.

ISHMAEL REED: *You were nine when you first picked up the horn?*

DAVID MURRAY: Yeah, I was born in 1955.

ISHMAEL REED: *Did you start with the alto?*

DAVID MURRAY: Yes, I played alto before I played tenor saxophone. But Mr. Hartman gave me my first horn. My mother and father met at Ephesians because my mother was the musical director in Fresno Church. She would come up to Ephesians to get new music and then take it back to her choir. That's how my mother and father met. In fact, my father learned guitar so he could sit next to her. That's how that went. One of the assistant pastors at Ephesians was Reverend Thurland Daniels. Reverend Thurland Daniels, my father, my mother and Sister Mills started the Missionary Church of God in Christ.

ISHMAEL REED: *Where was that located?*

DAVID MURRAY: It eventually was on Byron and Allston, down in Berkeley.

ISHMAEL REED: *So wait a minute, he gave you the alto that day?*

DAVID MURRAY: Yeah, Mr. Hartman gave it to me that day. I played it that night.

ISHMAEL REED: *Do you remember the date?*

DAVID MURRAY: No, I don't remember the date, but I remember that everyone said, "Wow, wow." I knew the songs because I was playing bongos along with them before I got the horn. I knew I wanted the saxophone.

ISHMAEL REED: *The Church of God in Christ?*

DAVID MURRAY: The Church of God in Christ. Yeah, it was Pentecostal.

ISHMAEL REED: *Were there drums and all that?*

DAVID MURRAY: My brother played clarinet and my cousin played trumpet, so it was natural that I wanted a saxophone. I played it that night and people said, "That's a lot of squeaking." (*Laughter*). I played three to four nights a week with my parents. The church wasn't happening unless my mother was there because she provided music. We had to go to church three nights a week and I kind of used that to play in between school. I was at Longfellow.

ISHMAEL REED: *Longfellow?*

DAVID MURRAY: It is now Longfellow Middle School. I passed by it the other day. Anyway, a couple of weeks later, and because nobody said anything bad, I continued to play the horn. I was trying to play the songs the first day, but I couldn't get the fingers down. That's why the horn would squeak. But I got better, and even now some people say I'm still squeaking, but I know where the squeaks are going. Back then, I couldn't control the squeaks, you know. Now we call it multiphonic. (*Laughter*).

ISHMAEL REED: *Spell it. I don't know what it means. A what?*

DAVID MURRAY: A multiphonic.

ISHMAEL REED: *Okay, okay. That's great. Okay. When did you get introduced to jazz? Did you have any jazz records around the house?*

DAVID MURRAY: Yeah, but I couldn't play them.

ISHMAEL REED: *What did you have? What did your parents have?*

DAVID MURRAY: Well, we were only allowed to listen to gospel music in the house.

ISHMAEL REED: *Did you listen to it on the radio?*

DAVID MURRAY: Yeah, at my friend's house.

ISHMAEL REED: *Well, what kind of music did you listen to?*

DAVID MURRAY: Let me explain. It wasn't until after my mother died...

ISHMAEL REED: *When was that?*

DAVID MURRAY: I was thirteen at that point. It must have been 1968. She wouldn't permit us to play jazz. The first record I got was *Blues Saxophones* by Coleman Hawkins and Ben Webster. I also had a couple of compilation records. I had a Stan Getz record and a Count Basie. Then I saw Sonny Rollins. A friend of mine took me to the Berkeley Jazz Festival. He made a deep impression. He had a saxophone that was bigger than the one I had and I knew about the tenor then but I had never heard someone bring that kind of sound and personality to the horns.

ISHMAEL REED: *Did he play for a long time that night?*

DAVID MURRAY: I don't think that they let him play that long, but he could have, on this occasion, because he didn't have a band. I don't know what happened. I was glad to be there. I remember coming home and telling my father, "This cat Sonny Rollins had this horn that was bigger than mine and it really spoke and I really want that horn." So we went and found out how much the horn cost. We went to this music store up there on Shattuck.

ISHMAEL REED: *Tupper and Reed.*

DAVID MURRAY: I guess so. It's the one that is now down there on University. I ended up taking clarinet lessons there a few years later. My father took me up to the credit union across from City Hall. He got me into the credit union so I could borrow some money to pay for this Selmer Mark tenor saxophone. It was very nice. It was brand new at the time and I bought it and paid for it with the few gigs I was doing.

ISHMAEL REED: *You were doing gigs?*

DAVID MURRAY: I was doing gigs already.

ISHMAEL REED: *And you were twelve? Like where?*

DAVID MURRAY: I had really steady gigs. We played a tour of all of the Shakey's Pizza Parlors in the Bay Area. I had a jazz trio. There was a drummer, an organ player, Charles Green, and me. We had a good show. We weren't really jazz musicians yet, but we would jazz up songs like *A Taste of Honey*. We were trying to play the blues and we were looking for information. We would hear a record that we liked and we would practice it. I think that really helped me to get to where I am today because I was playing in front of all of these people all of the time. Charles Green's mother was the principal of Frick School way out in East Oakland and we used to play these gigs and Charles Green played the keys, looking like Smokey Robinson. He was a great singer too. He was light-skinned and all of the girls liked him. Anyway, we would bust into some jazz during any point of the show. We were a hit.

ISHMAEL REED: *Great. How long did that last?*

DAVID MURRAY: Throughout junior high school. Seventh and eighth grade.

ISHMAEL REED: *Did you get paid?*

DAVID MURRAY: Yeah, we made money. I paid back the money for my saxophone even faster than a year. I had the best saxophone on the planet.

ISHMAEL REED: *And you were twelve?*

DAVID MURRAY: Yeah.

ISHMAEL REED: *And you had credit and you paid the saxophone off?*

DAVID MURRAY: Yeah, because my father didn't want to loan me the money. He took me to the credit union. That's how he knew I was going to pay for it, which was a good move.

ISHMAEL REED: *So your parents were really conscious of finances and budgeting?*

DAVID MURRAY: Well, conscious is not the word. They used to live out of this drawer with envelopes. Every Monday night they would huddle around this envelope drawer. My father was a garbage man for the City of Berkeley.

ISHMAEL REED: *You grew up in a middle-class home?*

DAVID MURRAY: Middle class? No. We were trying to be middle class. We weren't middle class. My father used to do everything he could. I remember days we would have to collect brass and other days where we would have to collect other metals and take it down to the junk-yard and do this and do that. He had us working the whole time and didn't want us to live in Oakland. He was very adamant about that because he worked all of his life so we could live on Stuart Street in Berkeley. He said, "I don't want you living over there" because during that time Oakland was not the proud city that it is now.

ISHMAEL REED: *What was your father's middle name?*

DAVID MURRAY: Walter Pendelton Murray.

ISHMAEL REED: *Did you experience any segregation? Joe Overstreet, famous African American painter who also grew up in Oakland, told me about neighborhoods you couldn't go to during those days. You came after Joe ...*

DAVID MURRAY: Well, I experienced plenty of racism, sure.

ISHMAEL REED: *In Oakland?*

DAVID MURRAY: In Oakland and Berkeley. Probably even more so in Berkeley than in Oakland.

ISHMAEL REED: *Like what?*

DAVID MURRAY: Well, you know, not being able to enter certain stores. I remember my mother not being able to go into stores to try on different dresses. There is still a lot of racism going on.

CARLA BLANK (*a dancer, choreographer and director, is Ishmael Reed's wife*): What about Berkeley High? Did they try and put you into a different program?

David Murray: Not really. I went to West Campus of Berkeley High in ninth grade, which was where all of the ninth graders were at the time. I also went to Willard Junior High School and Saint Mary's. I never had racism problems in school, in fact, I was a motivated student and I was always at the top. I was popular.

ISHMAEL REED: *You got good grades?*

DAVID MURRAY: Yeah, I never had that kind of problem. Maybe some of my friends did, but I never had that kind of problem. I was pretty popular. I had my band and sports.

ISHMAEL REED: *So, you played in high school?*

DAVID MURRAY: Yeah, but some of my friends that were not particularly motivated, you know, lived over on Ellis Street. I had a friend who would drive a Cadillac to school even though he wasn't old enough to drive and he had a gun. One of the funniest things that ever happened—well it may not seem funny—we were supposed to go to San Francisco to see *Hamlet* and the homeroom lady asked, "Does everyone have $2.50 for their snack at the theatre?" Robert Porter said, "$250? I keeps $250." He thought she was talking about $250. He was twelve.

ISHMAEL REED: *So when did you decide this was going to be your career?*

DAVID MURRAY: It was probably when I saw Sonny Rollins.

ISHMAEL REED: *I told him that you admired him.*

DAVID MURRAY: Of course, I told him that myself. I never really questioned what I was going to be, only how soon it was going to happen. I really didn't have another idea.

ISHMAEL REED: *Did you ever have any recordings out here?*

DAVID MURRAY: No, not really.

ISHMAEL REED: *So what happened down there in Claremont?*

DAVID MURRAY: I got a California state scholarship to go there. That was helpful.

ISHMAEL REED: *Did you play down there?*

DAVID MURRAY: Yeah, I did. The first week I got there I got a gig with an organ trio. An old guy had a rhythm box and he played an organ and sometimes the guitar player would show up but they needed a saxophone player. I had played at the California Hotel with Charles Brown so I had a little experience. Charles, you know, was a nice cat, maybe too nice, if you knew Charles Brown. Did you know Charles Brown?

ISHMAEL REED: *Yeah, I knew Charles Brown. He liked the racetrack a lot.*

DAVID MURRAY: Yeah, he liked the racetrack.

ISHMAEL REED: *I saw him at Neldon's Bakery. We had hired him for a gig and the woman we assigned to host him didn't know who he was and so she forgot to pick him up. I raced over to the Harriet Tubman Senior Citizens' home where he was living and he was waiting patiently. I raced him over to the Great American Music Hall and because publishers and their staff were attending the American Book Awards, there were about a thousand people in the audience. He got a standing ovation. Much later, when I saw him performing on the piano for the Oakland Symphony, he traced his comeback to that event.*

DAVID MURRAY: Oh, yeah, he was a legend here. He played with some of my friends. We were just kids learning how to play jazz and played with popular black musicians as well as hippie gigs. If we had stayed together, we may have turned out better than Frankie Beverly and Maze. When I left for New York I tried to get cats like Ranzell Merritt, Pookey Jenkins and Stanley Franks to come with me, but they didn't want to go.

ISHMAEL REED: *They were scared.*

DAVID MURRAY: They were scared of New York. Ranzell had to take care of his family because his mother had passed away. God bless her, his mother was a wonderful woman. She raised four kids by herself. My mother had already been dead for a while and my father was about to get remarried, so I couldn't wait to leave here if you want to know the truth. I love the Bay Area and in some ways I wish I hadn't left because it is a kind of paradise. The weather is perfect.

ISHMAEL REED: *Mike Gold, the communist writer, compared California to a sanitarium.*

DAVID MURRAY: Yeah, at the same time people pay money to go to the Mediterranean because it's the same climate as here. In any case, my calling was away from here.

ISHMAEL REED: *So how much money did you have when you landed in New York?*

DAVID MURRAY: How much money did I have? It was February and I had enough money to last until September.

ISHMAEL REED: *Did you have any relatives there?*

DAVID MURRAY: No. I knew Ray Anderson, a famous trombone player. I went to his house first. I stayed with Ray Anderson for about a month. He put me up on 6th Street in a tiny apartment. He was gracious enough to let me stay there, but it was crazy and I had to get out of there. Then I found an apartment.

ISHMAEL REED: *Where?*

DAVID MURRAY: It was on 103rd Street and Amsterdam. It ended up being with two junkies. I didn't know it at the time. They were upper middle-class junkies with rich parents.

ISHMAEL REED: *Were you roommates with them?*

DAVID MURRAY: Yes, I had a room in their apartment.

ISHMAEL REED: *What was that like?*

DAVID MURRAY: Well, I came home once and the chick had taken out my saxophone. She was playing with it and I said, "you can't be playing my saxophone." She said, "Well, help me tie up so I can shoot up." And I said, "I don't want to, I like to smoke weed." But I wasn't really into the drugs. Finally I got a lock on my door.

ISHMAEL REED: *Did you do any of those drugs?*

DAVID MURRAY: Oh, no. I wasn't into that kind of stuff. In California I was into psychedelic stuff. It was a California thing. I did reefers.

ISHMAEL REED: *So how long did you stay on 103rd?*

DAVID MURRAY: I stayed there until I could find another apartment. I lived everywhere on the Lower East Side. It was easy to get an apartment then. The rent was $150-$200 then. I don't know how young people do it now. Look, I had a spot for $200 right around 207 East 5th Street, near Amiri Baraka, Archie Shepp and all those cats near the Bowery. It was a great place to practice. It was cool. The only reason I had moved was because an animal had died up under me and that drove me crazy. That was the only reason I moved. Ten years ago, I talked to the guy that used to live next door to me—it was $2,750. Now that same apartment is over $3,000.

ISHMAEL REED: *So you met Stanley Crouch at Pomona College?*

DAVID MURRAY: Yeah, I met him around the same time that I met you.

ISHMAEL REED: *Where did you get a gig?*

DAVID MURRAY: I was playing with this trio. Then I got an extra gig that included a belly dancer. She wanted me to accompany her. I said, "Well, what do you want me to do?" I had a soprano sax then and she said, "Watch my navel." She was about fifty and had it together. She could dance! I watched her navel and made up music. I got $50 more a night working with her. That was my money for food. That helped me get through college.

ISHMAEL REED: *Did you ask Ornette for money?*

DAVID MURRAY: I never asked nobody for money. That wasn't my thing. I still don't like asking people for money.

ISHMAEL REED: *What year was this?*

DAVID MURRAY: '75.

ISHMAEL REED: '75. *Who was the next big jazz musician you ran into?*

DAVID MURRAY: Well, when I arrived in New York, I was going through a thing where I didn't know what direction I wanted to go into musically. Ornette was kind of dormant during this time and played a lot of pool. There wasn't much music going on in the house. If you want to know the truth, he was biding his time. All we really did was talk. We hardly ever played at all. Then I knew James "Blood" Ulmer. When we hooked up we played music. We didn't talk. I started playing with Blood's band immediately.

ISHMAEL REED: *What did he play?*

DAVID MURRAY: He played guitar. He played with Ornette and I saw them play at the Keystone. Ornette had Blood on guitar and Billy Higgins on drums. They applied Ornette's "Harmolodics" approach to jazz. It was a great band.

ISHMAEL REED: *Has the theory of "Harmolodics" been written out somewhere?*

DAVID MURRAY: Yes, it is written out, but a good example of it can be heard in Ornette's piece "Skies of America," in which everyone reads the piano part and transposes the C chart for their instruments. I'm actually going to play and do a lecture with Ornette in London on June 13 in which some of these ideas will be fleshed out.

ISHMAEL REED: *David Murray's early years. Thank you.*

WHERE ARE THE "PIRATES" COMING FROM?

An Interview with Nuruddin Farah[1]

ISHMAEL REED: *Okay, I want to ask you about the jubilation in this country about the rescue of the captain of that ship from the pirates, from the so-called "pirates."* [Event that took place on April 12, 2009.] *So what is your reaction to that?*

NURUDDIN FARAH: Well, I don't know what to say about the jubilation; maybe it is understandable, given what happened: the life of a captain, a human life, saved. Even so, the current situation—young pirates going amuck and making the sea of Somalia unsafe: this most certainly does present more difficulties for a country working its way out of a long-lasting civil war, especially since the amount

---

1. Nuruddin Farah is one of the major African authors writing today and a leading figure on the world literary scene. He is the author of ten novels, including *From a Crooked Rib*, the acclaimed trilogies *Variations on the Theme of an African Dictatorship* and *Blood on the Sun*. A third trilogy includes the titles *Links, Knots* and *Crossbones*. His novels have been translated into seventeen languages and have won numerous awards. Farah was named 1998 laureate of the Neustadt International Prize for Literature, and he is widely considered to be a leading candidate for the Nobel Prize for Literature. He was Regents Lecturer at The University of California at Berkeley in Spring 2009. A version of this interview appeared in *Black Renaissance/Renaissance Noire*.

of ransom money they are said to receive is far less than what they collect in the end. The current situation, in short, is untenable, as it privileges a group of radical Islamists intent on taking over the reins of the state, even if the current president is an Islamist—albeit of the moderate variety.

ISHMAEL REED: *What is a moderate Islamist?*

NURUDDIN FARAH: A moderate Islamist is an Islamist willing to talk to everybody and who also wants peace, and who does not necessarily insist on strict Sharia code—in other words, the views of a moderate Islamist are unlike those of the Taliban. Now while some of us have hoped to recreate, reconstruct, reconfigure the state in a secularist vein, we are less pleased with a moderate Islamist prepared to engage in a dialogue about peace and reconciliation. The current president was the executive director of the Islamic Courts Unions, an umbrella organization of Islamists. The radical group, Al-Shabab, said to be allied to Al-Qaeda—I've seen no tangible evidence, even though their mode of operation is similar to Al-Qaeda's—belonged to the same group.

ISHMAEL REED: *What is the name of the current president?*

NURUDDIN FARAH: Sheik Sharif Ahmed.

ISHMAEL REED: *Was he elected?*

NURUDDIN FARAH: He was—in fact; he won the election held not in Mogadiscio (*aka Mogadishu*), the capital of Somalia, seen as too dangerous for such an undertaking, but in another neighboring, partly Somali-speaking territory, Djibouti, on the Red Sea. His being moderate was the primary attraction, a man intelligent enough to know that in this day and age you have to accept to work with everyone, secularists as well as diehard religionists.

ISHMAEL REED: *How old is he?*

NURUDDIN FARAH: He is in his early forties.

ISHMAEL REED: *You negotiated between this president and who?*

NURUDDIN FARAH: I met him for several hours—he was then the executive director of the umbrella under which the Islamists were organized—when I was in Somalia attempting to broker peace between that group, then in control of Mogadiscio and much of southern Somalia, and the president of the weak federal government—based at the time in a garrison town called Baidoa, three hundred and fifty kilometers from Mogadiscio. The Islamist groups had defeated the warlords, whom they chased out of their citadels, despite U.S. financial and military assistance. (The Islamists enjoyed popular support; the warlords, who had misruled the country ever since the collapse of the state structures, were seen as anathema to people's aspirations and were hated by everyone.) A lot has happened since my attempt to broker the peace in 2006. For one thing, Ethiopia invaded Somalia, allegedly at the behest, and with the connivance of the U.S. (I've heard it said that a U.S. official admitted to the U.S. providing the Ethiopians with military intelligence ahead of their invasion of Somalia to oust the Islamists from power. Again, I have no hard evidence to go on, but it is generally believed to be the case.) What is in no doubt, however, is that the then President Yusuf of Somalia had a big hand in inviting the Ethiopians. As a consequence, the Islamists fled and then regrouped, the organization's topnotch basing themselves in Eritrea, with the fighters waging an insurgency inside the country. Ethiopia felt compelled to withdraw its forces following the resignation of President Yusuf.

ISHMAEL REED: *Why did he resign?*

NURUDDIN FARAH: He was asked to step down, because he was seen as an obstacle to peace and reconciliation. Threatened with sanctions, denied visas to travel out of the country, and with all his assets abroad coming under the hammer, President Yusuf resigned. The concerted efforts to get him to leave worked, because the African Union and a handful of donor nations and all the countries neighboring Somalia were very supportive of these measures.

ISHMAEL REED: *Which countries are these?*

NURUDDIN FARAH: Kenya, Ethiopia, Djibouti, Uganda—all of them neighboring Somalia, and being members of the regional bloc known as IGAD (Intergovernmental Authority on Development). As a bloc, the IGAD countries report to the African Union, and it was they who recommended that President Yusuf be isolated and asked to resign. And he did, seeing no benefit in staying.

ISHMAEL REED: *Where is he now?*

NURUDDIN FARAH: He is in Yemen.

ISHMAEL REED: *Who were those who supported him? Where did he get his money from?*

NURUDDIN FARAH: Well, everybody supported him when he was elected into office in 2006. But he became an obstacle because he continued to quarrel with everyone.

ISHMAEL REED: *When did you leave?*

NURUDDIN FARAH: I left Somalia in 1974—to do a graduate degree in theatre in England.

ISHMAEL REED: *Okay... now... Were there stable governments, prosperity when you were growing up in Somalia?*

NURUDDIN FARAH: Well, my life is a bit more complicated, in that I was born at a time when several Somali-speaking territories were under colonial rule—Britain, Italy, France and Ethiopia. I was born in what had been Italian Somalia, but Italy had lost the territory to Britain, following the Second World War. At the time, my father worked as an interpreter for the British and he was transferred to the Ogaden, which would in three or four years become part of Ethiopia, in 1948. So I grew up and went to school in the Ogaden, the Somali-speaking part of Ethiopia.

ISHMAEL REED: *But, still did you witness—did you know of any prosperity or stable governments in Somalia when you were growing up?*

NURUDDIN FARAH: There were brief instances of prosperity, not a great deal. I thought of myself as a colonial when, as a Somali, I lived in Ethiopia, under the imperial yoke, a most cruel regime—that of Emperor Haile Selassie. It wasn't until we moved to Somalia as a family, following a border war between Somalia and Ethiopia over the Ogaden territory that I felt at peace, in comfortable harmony with my own identity. Somalia enjoyed stability, democracy, etc.

ISHMAEL REED: *Wait, so you're saying there was a stable government?*

NURUDDIN FARAH: Yes, there was a stable government from 1960-1969, then there was a military coup.

ISHMAEL REED: *Which year was that?*

NURUDDIN FARAH: In 1969, to be precise, the 21st of October, 1969.

ISHMAEL REED: *Who engineered the coup? Who backed the coup?*

NURUDDIN FARAH: The Soviet Union backed the coup. General Siad Barre, who would later claim to be socialist, led the coup, which brought him to power. He was a ruthless dictator—the very tyrant who threatened me with death if I ever set foot in Somalia; he would sentence me to death later.

ISHMAEL REED: *He sentenced you to death?*

NURUDDIN FARAH: Yes. In absentia.

ISHMAEL REED: *What did this kind of economic system produce?*

NURUDDIN FARAH: The irony of it is that his tyranny produced the semblance of economic stability—in the Soviet style—poorly run state-owned farms, that sort of thing.

ISHMAEL REED: *Were they required to learn the Russian language?*

NURUDDIN FARAH: No. When General Siad Barre came to power, the media of instruction were English, Italian and Arabic. However, two years after his arrival on the scene, he decreed that Somali be made the language of instruction—Somali, which until then had no script. He set up a committee to provide Somali with a script—something very revolutionary, something only a dictator could do and get away with; and he did. The country was doing not too badly when the dictator decided to invade Ethiopia militarily, with the purpose of recovering the Somali-speaking territory called the Ogaden.

ISHMAEL REED: *That's where you grew up?*

NURUDDIN FARAH: Yes.

ISHMAEL REED: *So he attacked to recover…*

NURUDDIN FARAH: To recover the Ogaden, the Somali-speaking territory under dispute between Somalia and Ethiopia. In the event, Somalia lost the war when, with the war still ongoing, the Soviets changed allies, dumping Somalia and going over to the Ethiopian side. Not only that, but they also entered the war and recruited Cuba to join too—to expel the Somali army from the Ogaden, almost all of it then in Somali hands. Defeated, the Somali National Army returned home. You could say that from then onwards, Somalia became a basket case—a nation that couldn't feed itself, a nation that relied on foreign food aid.

ISHMAEL REED: *So the Soviet Union switched sides?*

NURUDDIN FARAH: They switched sides.

ISHMAEL REED: *And they backed Ethiopia? They came and joined Ethiopia?*

NURUDDIN FARAH: After the debacle, General Siad Barre switched sides too. No longer a Soviet ally and no longer a socialist, he became a good friend of the U.S. And Ronald Reagan became his closest ally, arming Somalia with American weapons.

ISHMAEL REED: *After first becoming a friend of the Soviet Union, after the Soviet Union abandoned him?*

NURUDDIN FARAH: Yes.

ISHMAEL REED: *So both of these states were pawns between these Cold War powers?*

NURUDDIN FARAH: A pawn to the Soviets, then to the Americans— and what did Somalia gain? Our country gained the largest stash of hardware; weapons the Soviets provided to the Somali army were then supplemented by those the U.S. would supply. All this turned our country into a ticking bomb, which would explode—and it exploded in 1990.

ISHMAEL REED: *Well how many people were killed in the war between Somalia and Ethiopia? We're talking millions?*

NURUDDIN FARAH: We are.

ISHMAEL REED: *Because the Soviet Union and the United States, which would eventually reconcile, were engaged in a geopolitical chess game over there?*

NURUDDIN FARAH: Somalia, with the longest coastal line in Africa, is neighbor to the Middle East—and therefore strategic. You need to have Somalia to make sure you can gain easy, undeterred access to the Arabian Gulf and its oil wealth.

ISHMAEL REED: *So Yemen and Somalia are considered hotbeds of Al Qaeda activity, so if some nation was able to set up bases in Somalia they could run that whole area, right?*

NURUDDIN FARAH: Well, they could. But I doubt if anyone can establish bases there.

ISHMAEL REED: *Why?*

NURUDDIN FARAH: The country is so ungovernable. Moreover, the place is awash with weapons.

ISHMAEL REED: *When did Somalia become ungovernable and why?*

NURUDDIN FARAH: Somalia is ungovernable, because it is awash with weapons from the Soviet and the Reagan eras.

ISHMAEL REED: *The neo-cons were doing the same thing in Mozambique, right?*

NURUDDIN FARAH: There you are.

ISHMAEL REED: *What were you trying to achieve when you engaged in this diplomatic effort and who asked you to do it?*

NURUDDIN FARAH: Nobody asked me to do it.

ISHMAEL REED: *You volunteered?*

NURUDDIN FARAH: I was between two novels and I thought I could be of some use—brokering peace between the fighting groups in Somalia.

ISHMAEL REED: *What novels were you in between?*

NURUDDIN FARAH: I was between the latest novel, *Knots* and the one I am writing [*Crossbones*].

ISHMAEL REED: *Do you have a title for the new novel?*

NURUDDIN FARAH: No, I don't. Not yet.

ISHMAEL REED: *So how did you find the time to write novels while you were doing all of this negotiating and traveling?*

NURUDDIN FARAH: Well, it's a bit difficult to write and at the same negotiate and travel.

ISHMAEL REED: *So, back to the "failed state," which is the language they use over here, Reagan's intervening on the side of the dictator— did this contribute to the failed state?*

NURUDDIN FARAH: Most definitely.

ISHMAEL REED: *So what do people do for money? What is their every-day life? How do they get their food?*

NURUDDIN FARAH: People lead hand-to-mouth existence, many rely-ing on the remittances from their relatives in Europe and North America. The only groups who do very well and who need not wait for remittances are the armed groups: these engage in daily robber-ies, and hold the entire population hostage.

ISHMAEL REED: *Are you saying the whole country is armed?*

NURUDDIN FARAH: The whole country is awash with guns.

ISHMAEL REED: *So, if a family is sending their children to school what would happen?*

NURUDDIN FARAH: They would have to have a gun or allies of theirs who are armed.

ISHMAEL REED: *So, is there some kind of protection racket going on there?*

NURUDDIN FARAH: The last time I was in Mogadiscio, I had to have armed escorts to go round. Otherwise, you could be hijacked or even killed.

ISHMAEL REED: *So if I'm a family, and I want some protection, do I pay somebody?*

NURUDDIN FARAH: One way is to have bodyguards; the other is to have the guns yourself.

ISHMAEL REED: *So there's a bodyguard industry?*

NURUDDIN FARAH: You would hire armed security who would stand at the gate daily, every minute of the day, checking who is coming in and going out.

ISHMAEL REED: *So what about schools and health care?*

NURUDDIN FARAH: The schools are taught in Arabic, because charitable Arab organizations provide the funds—and in addition to Arabic, the schools teach much religion too. This means that Somali has been reduced to a second language. The hospitals are in a bad way too—run with the financial assistance of the Red Cross, Red Crescent, UNICEF, etc.

ISHMAEL REED: *So the Arabs are asserting influence in Somalia?*

NURUDDIN FARAH: They are asserting negative influence, changing the position of our mother tongue, the Somali language, and making it into a second language.

ISHMAEL REED: *And the Russians didn't even do that, right?*

NURUDDIN FARAH: The Russians couldn't succeed where the Arabs have done. Because Somalia is now a failed state and the Arabs pay the salaries of the teachers, pay for the blackboards and the chalk, and they say that you must teach in Arabic. The curriculum has also changed. The curriculum is that of an Arabic curriculum.

ISHMAEL REED: *Is there a conflict between the Arabs attempting to assert control in Africa and the artists and intellectuals? I hear this from people like Wole Soyinka and Chinwezu and Ousemane.*

NURUDDIN FARAH: There has always been a conflict. But in the end, victory goes to the one with stashes of money.

ISHMAEL REED: *You guys have intellect and a worldwide audience. That must count for something.*

NURUDDIN FARAH: Well, sure.

ISHMAEL REED: *How do the rich get by?*

NURUDDIN FARAH: The rich people become richer, they hire more gunmen so they can acquire more and then protect what they have got by illegal means.

ISHMAEL REED: *How do they get their money?*

NURUDDIN FARAH: Through corruption and coercion.

ISHMAEL REED: *What about the middle class?*

NURUDDIN FARAH: The middle classes flee war zones and become refugees in other lands.

ISHMAEL REED: *So you have rich people who like what their situation is?*

NURUDDIN FARAH: The rich run the rackets, and the middle classes and the poor are their daily victims. They like the current civil war situation.

ISHMAEL REED: *What I meant to say was that the rich people like the situation and the poor people are desperate? Is there a class conflict going on there?*

NURUDDIN FARAH: We can use terms like "class" in a situation in which a hungry man desperate for a meal extends his hand, begging.

Such a hungry man is prepared to worship the rich if the rich will feed him.

ISHMAEL REED: *So where do the rich people live? Do they live in a certain section of the country?*

NURUDDIN FARAH: They live in Mogadiscio, but they are protected.

ISHMAEL REED: *And they have resorts there that they go to?*

NURUDDIN FARAH: No, because the majority of the people who are now rich in Somalia are newcomers to the city and have not developed bourgeois lifestyles.

ISHMAEL REED: *No, resorts, like vacation places.*

NURUDDIN FARAH: They go to Kenya and Europe.

ISHMAEL REED: *Okay, now I got the* Guardian *article and it says that the pirates were socialists in the old days, they rescued African slaves— Who's dumping nuclear wastes? I saw the blogs.*

NURUDDIN FARAH: A number of the European Union countries are; supposedly, allegedly, Italy and Germany. A number of the EU countries make arrangements with some of the warlords and they pay $10,000 to warlords to allot dumping sites for their waste companies.

ISHMAEL REED: *So the warlords sold us into slavery—they are still selling people in Africa?*

NURUDDIN FARAH: Sure. If you Google "dumping nuclear waste in Somalia" you will find lots of articles.

ISHMAEL REED: *The* Guardian *article also said that these "pirates" were people who went out to stop trawlers and stop the dumping?*

NURUDDIN FARAH: That was the original idea—to stop the waste dumping, and to protect the country's maritime resources. But there is a difference between the intentions of the fishing communities who were fighting against foreign illegal fishing and the young pirates whose main wish is to take hostages and collect ransom. Previously, when the fishermen apprehended a fishing vessel illegally fishing, they would fine the owners, make them pay damages, and they would put the money back into the community. They would distribute it among the fishermen so that they could continue to fish. Lately, young pirates have joined in to exploit an exploitable situation. A majority of the young pirates are not fishermen. That is the big difference. The other is that if and when they lay their hands on some of the ransom money—mind you, a lot of money does not reach the pirates; much of the money remains in Abu Dhabi, where the negotiators are based, and in London where the banks are—the pirates do not put a cent of it into the community. They blow it, they waste it—on cars, on prostitutes, on chewing qaat.

ISHMAEL REED: *So, some of it goes to banks?*

NURUDDIN FARAH: The money does not go to Somalia. I can assure you of that.

ISHMAEL REED: *I got a figure of 200 hostages. There are still hostages, yes?*

NURUDDIN FARAH: I do not know how low or high the hostage figures are.

ISHMAEL REED: *Does the money go to Al Qaeda?*

NURUDDIN FARAH: No idea.

ISHMAEL REED: *What about Al Shabab?*

NURUDDIN FARAH: Al Shabab are fighting in Mogadiscio.

ISHMAEL REED: *They are not pirates?*

NURUDDIN FARAH: They are not pirates.

ISHMAEL REED: *Is the United States involved in some kind of way?*

NURUDDIN FARAH: Not yet.

ISHMAEL REED: *They're not in Somalia? They don't have drones there?*

NURUDDIN FARAH: Not yet.

NURUDDIN FARAH: Al-Shabab would shoot anybody who supports the government because they want to overthrow the government.

ISHMAEL REED: *Where does the historical antipathy between Somalia and Ethiopia come from? What's the origin of that?*

NURUDDIN FARAH: It is age-old—the enmity between Somalia and Ethiopia.

ISHMAEL REED: *Over religion?*

NURUDDIN FARAH: There is that particular love/hate relationship between neighbors. Ethiopia seems to have benefited from being Christian—a Christian island in an Islamic ocean—and Somalis seem to have been victims, because they are Muslim.

ISHMAEL REED: *What about intermarriage between Ethiopia and Somalia?*

NURUDDIN FARAH: They marry one another's women. That's not difficult.

ISHMAEL REED: *Are there a lot of instances of that?*

NURUDDIN FARAH: Yeah, yeah, yeah.

ISHMAEL REED: *Now the right wing is saying that Obama's not a wuss any longer, he is not a wimp. He belongs to a real macho club, now. After having had those pirates shot.*

NURUDDIN FARAH: I am glad that the captain has been released unharmed. I wish something could be done about the pirates, because they are complicating a very complicated issue.

ISHMAEL REED: *Well, what would you do?*

NURUDDIN FARAH: Well, I would support the autonomist state of Puntland.

ISHMAEL REED: *Where is that state located?*

NURUDDIN FARAH: It is part of Somalia, but it is in the northeast.

ISHMAEL REED: *They've always wanted autonomy?*

NURUDDIN FARAH: No, it became autonomous when the country collapsed in the Civil War.

ISHMAEL REED: *Why would you think that would be the solution?*

NURUDDIN FARAH: Because the largest number of pirates are local to Puntland, and only the people of Puntland would know how to deal with them. You need to train the soldiers, train them so they can patrol the seas and the coastal areas on land too. The pirates aren't helping anyone, not even themselves.

The U.S. Puts Its Best Foot Forward[1]

The August 20, 2010 press release came from Jorn Weisbrodt, then executive director of Robert Wilson Works:

> Over a year ago Robert Wilson was asked to participate as artistic director for the event celebrating the thirtieth anniversary of Solidarnosc, the freedom movement that started the fall of the iron curtain. It will be on August 31 in the historic shipyards in Gdansk and is free to the public. I hope that you can join and spread the news.

The other press release came from the European Solidarity Centre:

> On behalf of Polish President Lech Walesa and the European Solidarity Centre in Poland I would like to invite you to participate in a unique initiative.
>
> This year on August 31 we will be celebrating the thirtieth anniversary of the establishment of the Solidarity movement which fought for freedom, dignity and human rights. In 2005 the European Parliament

---

1. Ishmael Reed was artist in residence in the summer of 2009, when this 2010 event was being planned. He was able to observe some of the goings-on at this hub of artistic global activity. At a time when Anti-Muslim Neo-Nativists are embarrassing the United States by exhibiting their ignorant behinds, American artists once again show our country at its best, its noblest, its highest spirit. A version of this essay appeared at Counterpunch.org, August 30, 2010.

decided that 31 August is to be celebrated as the *Day of Freedom and Solidarity*. That is why we have launched an extraordinary initiative— before and on that day we would like some most important people in Poland and around the world to wear the historic "Solidarnosc" badge as a symbol of our solidarity with people from all over the world who are still deprived of freedom, peace and prosperity.

Please also accept our warm invitation to the spectacular show prepared by world famous American artist Robert Wilson which will take place on August 31 in Poland at the Gdansk Shipyard, the birthplace of the Solidarity Movement. If you wish to participate in this event please click HERE for more information. As the event will be attended by government officials including the President of Poland, there are serious security measures.

Yours sincerely,
Lech Walesa
European Solidarity Centre

Though some of the senators who grilled Supreme Court Justice Sotomayor and the American media, up to its old tricks by raising lynch mobs against misunderstood groups, might have problems with diversity, white European and American artists, regardless of their motives, have drawn materials from a variety of cultures for at least one hundred years. Like those senators, many art critics and academics lack the intellectual curiosity of the artist and refuse to acknowledge the contributions of the world cultures to western art. The kind of people who call Picasso's work "Cubist" as a way of denying its African influences.

The private art collections of Picasso and surrealist Andre Breton are filled with art from Africa and the Pacific Islands. So is Robert Wilson's. Louis Aragon said of Wilson that he was continuing Surrealism's traditions.

The art that was once labeled "primitive" is located in the basement of the main building of Watermill, a community of artists directed by Robert Wilson. Other parts of the collection are dispersed throughout the building and unlike the way that museums might distance their exhibits from the presence of the viewer, the art—chairs, tables, bowls, etc.—is blended into the day's routine. Precious lamps or chairs might be part of the office furniture.

Among pieces in the collection are footwear that once belonged to Rudolph Nureyev and Marlene Dietrich. Jerome Robbins' cool sneakers are on display. I wore mine. Unlike some of the tourists that my daughter Tennessee and I spotted in the lobby of a San Francisco hotel, who were freezing in their light summer clothing, I was prepared for New York's hot and muggy August weather. I spent six years during New York Augusts like the 2009 August. I arrived packed with Hawaiian shirts, two of which were sewn by a reader who lives in Hilo. Me and Truman.

Wilson's art collection is located at the Watermill Center, founded in 1992 by Wilson. It is described as an international, multi-disciplinary center for studies in the arts and humanities. Wilson is best known for large-scale multimedia works, the most famous of which are *Einstein on the Beach* and *the CIVIL WarS*. One of his most recent works is *KOOL, Dancing in my Mind*, based upon collaborations between Wilson, my partner, Oakland choreographer and author Carla Blank, and the great Japanese dancer and choreographer Suzushi Hanayagi.

Most of the *KOOL* background music is provided by David Byrne. It is a multimedia work in which six dancers perform, two of whom are Merce Cunningham alumni. Blank also did the research and dramaturge for the work that premiered at the Guggenheim Museum in April 2009, and was reworked and performed on August 8 and 9 of that year at Guild Hall in East Hampton, a town in which there are buildings that date to the 1600s. The Huffington Post called the work "sublime."

KOOL is in part a tribute to Ms. Hanayagi, now living in a Tokyo nursing home, suffering from Alzheimer's.

I suggested the title *KOOL* based upon my study of Japanese. I found that Suzushi meant cool, which certainly describes Suzushi's temperament. I'd known her since the 1960s, and never did I see her raise her voice or go hot.

Next stops for *KOOL* were the Akademie der Kunste, in Berlin, September 12, 2010. Richard Rutkowski's twenty-six-minute film based on the work was also to be shown there on August 25. *KOOL* also happened on December 9 at the Jerome Robbins Theater at the Baryshnikov Arts Center in New York City.

Rutkowski's projections, which are part of this multimedia work, were made in 2008 when Wilson, Blank and Rutkowski traveled to Osaka, where they visited Ms. Hanayagi. As a result, her powerful and poignant presence looms over the six dancers.

KOOL is just one of the projects that was undertaken by Watermill in 2009. The Watermill Center is a hub of creativity for artists from Europe, the Americas, Asia and the Pacific. Among them are up to 75 participants from over 22 countries, ranging from Israel, Taiwan, Indonesia, to Germany, Denmark, and Mexico.

According to Sue Jane Stoker, the summer program director:

> About 45-50 young artists are not attached to any specific project and there are about 20-25 more mature artists who come for a specific project or projects.

Among the projects, according to Sue Jane, are the:

> Staging of *Il Ritorno d'Ulisse in Patria* (for La Scala, Milan) *The Makropulos Case* (for the National Theater of Prague), *A Very Dark Matter* (new theater piece with music by Tom Waits, based on the life of Hans Christian Anderson), *Hakame, Footprints in the Sand* (theater work, maybe film), *Don Juan Tenorio* (theater work for Valladoid, Spain), Gdansk Poland, Thirtieth Anniversary Celebration of Beginning of Solidarity Movement, *The Wanderer* (film based on the lives of three generations of Wyeth Painters), concept development for an exhibition of the Watermill Collection, concept development and staging for *Light Leaves* (theater piece for the University of Iowa).

As soon as one group departs another flies in to work on projects with Wilson and his co-workers. I overheard chatter about the projects while standing in the buffet line, where guests were fed with meals designed by Malaysians Zowita Mustapha and Julie Tan. The menu for two days:

On August 8: Malaysian chicken satay and beef satay served with a spicy peanut sauce and ketupat (steamed compressed rice cakes that go well with the peanut sauce). There was also some deep-fried tofu for the vegetarians and that was served with the peanut sauce as well as another spicy chili sauce.

The August 9 Sunday Brunch was smoked salmon with capers and red onions, platters of assorted cheeses, assorted fruit boats, scrambled eggs, vegetable frittata, assorted sausages, roasted potatoes, bread baskets, and mixed greens with a balsamic mustard and honey vinaigrette.

During the daily meetings, the participants sat on the floor on four sides of a long room. Before Wilson entered, his assistant, Sue Jane Stoker, who besides being the summer program director is also the assistant director and stage manager for *KOOL*, went over some housekeeping duties for the participants. I asked Sue Jane about some of the issues covered the day that I attended a meeting.

On the 9th, as it was a Sunday, we would have reminded people that there is no dinner provided that evening and they get a $15 meal stipend. We talked about who are the guests who will be at lunch (that day it was a couple of people from the original school of Byrds, Bob's original group back in the 60s). Go over who will help in the kitchen, in the garden, if there are carpentry projects or art collection projects that need help, who will do the recycling (always Shang!), and because there were people leaving that day we remind people that when they leave, they should make sure that they change the sheets on their bed and leave clean sheets and towels for the next person coming in.

Not just the young artists, everyone who participates (including me)— each person is part of a group, and once a week, each group does the following: breakfast clean up, van clean up, toilet clean up, lunch clean up, office clean up, dinner clean up.

In Rutkowski's film about the making of *KOOL*, there appears a scene of Wilson on a Tokyo train. Slim, suited up and bespectacled, he could be a banker or math teacher. This older fuller Wilson, who enters the room at the conclusion of Ms. Stoker's remarks, is wearing a black T-shirt and pants.

I've been brought here to read from my poetry and to discuss my work with vocalists including Cassandra Wilson and Taj Mahal. In Rutkowski's film, I'm the one who is singing. Toward the end of her career, Suzushi Hanayagi, as part of a Tokyo solo concert, performed to music from *Conjure*, the CD produced by Kip Hanrahan on which musicians set my words to music. As a gag, I sang "Minnie the Moocher," a song made famous by Cab Calloway. The portion of her concert in which she used the song is part of the film.

After introducing me, Wilson asked me to sing it but it had been so long that I didn't remember anything beyond the first few lines and so Sue Jane had to fill in. I thanked her and she said, "No problem, I've been listening to the song every night." Wilson began the session with a silence, which invited the assembled artists to engage in meditation. He then rose and selected four people from the group, including Carla Blank. They began an impromptu movement piece. He bade farewell to a group that had been working on *The Makropulos Case*. They had to catch a plane to Prague. Two people, whose project was *A Very Dark Matter*, were leaving for Germany.

Wilson saluted another dancer from Greece for her work during the summer. Her name is Mariana Kavallie Ratos. She was applauded and she responded with tears. After the meeting, he took us to a room whose floor is covered with stones taken from riverbeds. He discussed his philosophy of architecture, one based upon simplicity. Simplicity is the approach here. Artists at Watermill make do with what is available. They live in dorm-like cubicles or share space in rented houses.

Later, during a tour of the Watermill's art collection, Sherry Dobbin, Watermill Center's program director, pointed to an installation located among the trees done by a Japanese artist using only rope. The rope cost $50.00. After the tour, we're told that if we're silent we could watch a rehearsal of Claudio Monteverdi's *Il Ritorno d'Ulisse in Patria*. It was presided over by the stern eye of Ellen Hammer, the dramaturgist. Wilson instructed the dancers. She was assisted by two young men who followed the dance notations. Wilson requested that I sit in a throne-like chair. It consisted of red and black blocks. Later I learned that it was designed by an Italian Futurist.

While I followed the rehearsal of a work that is to be performed in Milan, two years from now, I glanced across the path to what remains of a forest where on a deck, Yuki Kawahisa, a *KOOL* dancer was doing her warm ups. The small forest is dotted with stone monoliths brought from Indonesia. Performances seemed to constantly spring up on the grounds– grounds that are generously landscaped with pastures of grasses, ferns, pines.

At lunch, Meg Harper, one of the *KOOL* dancers, introduced me to Ritty Burchfield who was with Wilson in the early days. The days before *Einstein on the Beach*, the opera with music composed by Phil Glass. This was the work that established Wilson's reputation in the United States. Burchfield says that it had been established earlier in Europe with *Deafman Glance*, which was influenced by an autistic black youngster named Raymond Andrew. Burchfield performed in some of Wilson's works including *Life and Times of Joe Stalin*.

Another autistic collaborator is Christopher Knowles, who influenced *Einstein on the Beach*. I was standing next to him in the chow line. I asked him "What is your role here?"

"My role," he answered. "I don't know what you mean. I'm an artist," which really put me in my place. Knowles was consultant for the movie *Rain Man*. Later Wilson showed me some of Knowles's prose that your average Language poet would give their eyeteeth to write. (Wilson was born with learning disabilities. The son of a mayor of Waco, Texas, he didn't speak until he was five.)

Burchfield was John Cage's "roadie." She says that the possibilities of American dance have been expanded as more players participate. She watches popular dance shows like *So You Think That You Can Dance*. She says that hip-hop dancers are doing moves like triple flips that ballet dancers would envy.

As an example of how everybody pitched in, whether it be cleaning toilets or driving visitors to and fro from their houses, Carla and I were transported to our guest house in the woods by Aram Hausi-Rahbari, who collaborated on several operas including *Mary Queen of Scots* and *The Makropulos Case*. Driving these roads at night reminded me of the final scene in *Pollack* when Jackson Pollack, an early Hampton resident and his terrified passengers are headed for a crash.

Among those who were passengers on our return trip to the center was Illenk Gentille, who also performed in *KOOL*. A dancer from Sulawesi, Indonesia, he gave us an impromptu lecture on Indonesian court dance as we returned to the Center where brain-storming was taking place at different locations.

I even found myself pitching in. Though I was invited to discuss my poetry and my work with musicians, it was requested that I stay longer. Wilson wanted me to participate in a session about a huge spectacular multimedia show that took place in Gdansk on August 31, to celebrate the thirtieth anniversary of Poland's Solidarity Movement. The estimated audience: 100,000. The plans for the show were presented on laptops and by a huge board covered with pictures.

Examining this display was Father Macie Jzieba, a Catholic priest, and former physicist, who recommended Wilson. "They wanted Madonna," he said. He presented a ten-minute video which showed Polish history from the Russian and Nazi occupations to the General Strike. On a sheet of paper, Wilson sketched the grounds where performances would be held. I recommended that Polish poets be used, including the work of Nobel Prize winner Czeslaw Milosz. Someone suggested two famous rock musicians to be part of the spectacular show. After I left, I sent a note suggesting the most famous Polish musician since Chopin: Lawrence Welk.

Jorn Weisbrodt, Wilson's creative director, troubleshooter and budget hawk, chimed in from time to time about costs. *KOOL* dancer Jonah Bokaer had drawn a sketch for possible sky writing.

Recommendations were flying throughout the meeting while Wilson sketched ideas for the fireworks, which I thought were the perfect image for what goes on at this productive multicultural community of artists. Thought fireworks from minds shooting off at every possible direction. Lighting up brains. During the 1930s there was a similar meeting of multicultural minds.

The right was responsible for closing down the Works Progress Administration (WPA), a program that put writers, dancers and actors on salary, some of whom would become our leading artists.

During one red-baiting session before a congressional committee, a congressman wanted to know, "Who is this Christopher Marlowe fellow?" Now a conservative group called Media Morality is objecting to stimulus funds being used to support the arts. The basis for this attitude seems to be that the arts have no value.

A comparatively low budget project like *KOOL*, a masterpiece, whose start-up budget was not more than $30,000, and which requires not much beyond its six performers, stage lighting, a floor to ceiling projection screen and a few sticks and a large ball, making it ready to travel throughout the world in these low budget times, drew full houses at both the Guggenheim and Guild Hall. I'm sure that the fledging restaurant businesses and other local businesses that benefited from the crowds drawn by this work would disagree with Media Morality. Ralph Ellison was one of those writers who was on the WPA payroll. Publishing corporations have made millions over the years from his work, written during his time on a WPA payroll. His book, *Invisible Man*, is still in print.

Thousands of artists from all over the world have flocked to New York as a result of its becoming a world center for art, boosting the economy of the city as a result of the works by artists like Jackson Pollack, a recipient of a WPA salary. One of those who came to New York as a result of this artistic firmament was a young Japanese dancer named Suzushi Hanayagi.[2]

---

2. Both Suzushi Hanayagi and Sue Jane Stoker have since died.

More non-fiction from Baraka Books

Slouching Towards Sirte
NATO's War on Libya and Africa (forthcoming October 2012)
Maximilian C. Forte

Barack Obama and the Jim Crow Media
The Return of the Nigger Breakers
Ishmael Reed

The First Jews in North America 1760-1860
The Extraordinary Story of the Hart Family
Denis Vaugeois

A People's History of Quebec
Jacques Lacoursière & Robin Philpot

An Independent Quebec
The past, the present and the future
Jacques Parizeau, former Premier of Quebec

Trudeau's Darkest Hour
War Measures in Time of Peace, October 1970
Edited by Guy Bouthillier & Édouard Cloutier

The Question of Separatism
Quebec and the Struggle over Sovereignty
Jane Jacobs

Soldiers for Sale
German "Mercenaries" with the British in Canada during
the American Revolution 1776-83
Jean Pierre Wilhelmy

America's Gift
What the World Owes to the Americas and Their First Inhabitants
Käthe Roth and Denis Vaugeois